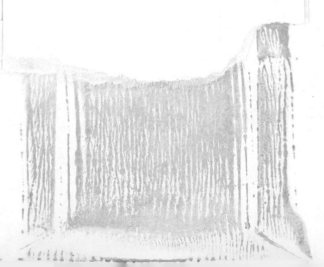

Other Books by Jerry Sohl

Underhanded Bridge

BY JERRY SOHL

A Hilarious Handbook of Devious Diversions and Stratagems for Winning at Bridge

Illustrated by Roy Schlemme

HAWTHORN BOOKS, INC.
PUBLISHERS/New York

UNDERHANDED BRIDGE

Library of Congress Catalog Card Number: 74–15639

ISBN: 0–8015–8128–1

2 3 4 5 6 7 8 9 10

Contents

Underhanded Bridge

1
Is Nothing Sacred?

A Fistful of Spades

There is a place in the heart of Los Angeles called the Magic Castle. It is really castlelike, difficult to reach if you've never been there before, and it is a sort of retreat for magicians. Yet it is more than that, for people in show business—stars, producers, writers, designers—and those in allied professions go there for dinner and to watch professional magicians do their thing in little amphitheaters.

On one of the nights I was there an older magician, whom I shall call Miles Evart, took his seat beside me at one of the big felt-covered tables and went through a series of astonishing card tricks—making entire decks vanish at will; causing cards to rise, fall, or float; dealing out perfect bridge hands—all of it appropriately electrifying and incredible.

There were a half dozen of us at the table watching him like hawks, but of course, we were unable to detect how these things could possibly be done. The overhead lights were bright, even dazzling. If I had not seen these things with my own eyes, I would have said they were impossible.

Near the end of his act Miles Evart turned to me and extended his hand with a deck of cards in it saying, "Examine these cards."

I took the cards, studied them carefully, fanned them to show them to those at the table, and held them up so that the others in the amphitheater seats could see. The cards were obviously an ordinary bridge deck with the cards arranged in no particular order. I wondered what kind of trick Evart was going to perform and vowed to learn its secret, whatever it was. After all, how could I miss anything with Evart only about two feet away from me?

He said, "Now hand the cards to me."

I held up the deck to him, slyly noting that a nine of diamonds was the bottom card and a three of spades the top. I was still holding the cards when Evart took hold of the deck with three fingers on top and his thumb on the bottom. His little finger did not touch the cards at all; it merely waggled in midair. I was about to release my hold and let him do with the cards what he would when he said, "Don't let go!"

I needed no encouragement. I gripped the cards hard. I told myself I'd *feel* whatever he was doing—*if* he could do anything. How could he? Wasn't I holding the cards, too?

He brought his eyes up to mine, smiled, and then said, "Do you want these cards?" He still had not released them and neither had I. "Just an ordinary pack, right?"

"Right."

"You could use them in your next bridge game. You do play bridge, don't you?"

"I sure do," I said, wondering what he was getting at.

"I think," Evart said, "that you'd better look at the cards

first." He let the pack go. "After you examine them, if you still want them, you're welcome to them."

I opened the cards, then spread them out on the felt for all to see.

Every card was a king of spades!

The Alcatraz Coup

It was at this moment that I realized that although I knew that (1) the Bangkok Club convention was developed by Somboon Nandhabiwat of Thailand and I was familiar with how to play it; (2) the probability of holding thirteen cards of the same suit in a bridge hand was .00000000016 percent, and; (3) that a two no trump response is positive for the Roman two diamonds, which indicates a strong three-suited hand, what I had just experienced rendered such fancy knowledge useless in any game wherein the opposition consisted of two Miles Evarts.

Of course there were no *two* Miles Evarts, but there had been others. Yes, I remembered other bridge rogues. Some had amused me, others had made me cry. Still others had caused me to gnash my teeth. Some I recalled fondly, some even with warm affection; others—even after all these years—still made me bristle.

There was Carter Lyndhurst, for example. He and his wife, Harriet, had come over for an evening of half a cent a point. My wife, Jean, and I were still young innocents adrift among a shoal of schemers then. Calvin was jovial. His wife was on the taciturn side, and a drink or two never loosened her up, even when she was dummy, as she was in this particular hand:

NORTH
A J 10

WEST   EAST
Q x   x x x

SOUTH
K x

Carter had to make three tricks or go down, so he, being South and the declarer, led the jack from dummy, Harriet looking on vacant-eyed (most beguilingly as I was to discover later). My wife, East, had no choice but to play a small card. I would cover with the queen if Carter played a small card, and his finesse through East for the queen would have failed.

South played a small card of another suit! I blinked. I thought I had counted right, but I was wrong. So I reached out to take the trick with the queen—except that I *didn't* take it because Carter, suddenly coming to his senses, said, "Oh, I've played the wrong suit!" and promptly took back his small card of the other suit and put on his king. He said to me, "You don't have to lose your queen, you know. You have the privilege of playing a smaller card if you have one of the suit."

So I played my small card, and Carter won with the king. Next he won my queen via the small card and the ace in dummy.

Tails I Win, Heads You Lose

It suddenly became clear to me that if, in the first place, I had played the small card of the suit being led from dummy instead of the queen, Carter would still have revoked, then substituting his failure to follow suit with the small card of the suit led, letting the jack win. Then he would have played to the king from dummy to capture my queen. His maneuver was merely one of determining where the queen was. And it was, as I found out, perfectly legal.

At the time, however, I didn't think so. I said, "Hey! That's not fair, Carter, you not following suit like that."

"Not *fair?*" Carter's eyebrows went up and his eyes became round with innocence. "Why isn't it fair?"

I had moxie enough to say, "A director or bridge committee would get you for that, Carter. They'd probably penalize you two tricks. In fact, I think you ought to take the loss anyway." Not following suit, indeed!

"Now just wait a minute, old buddy," Carter said. "You just don't know the rules." He withdrew from his coat pocket a copy of the *Laws of Contract Bridge.* * "Look here," he said, turning pages and finding what he wanted. He put the book on the table, his fingers pointing to Law 62: Correction of a Revoke.

It read, in part, ". . .[the revoke] may be replaced without penalty if it was played from the declarer's . . . hand. [A] member of the nonoffending side may, without penalty, withdraw any card he may have played after the revoke but before attention was drawn to it."

"It's fair," Carter said, beaming. "See? You were even able to save your queen."

"Yeah, only to have you take it on the next play."

Carter shrugged. "Those are the breaks, fella." Then, with a grin at the vacuous Harriet: "Things are tough all over."

It dawned on me then that had Harriet opened her mouth (I was certain she was aware of what was going on), she could have stopped the swindle.

* *Laws of Contact Bridge: The International Code* (New York: Crown, 1963).

"It's called the Alcatraz Coup," Carter said. "Surprised you didn't know that. Ought to try it some time." He started to shuffle the cards. Suddenly Harriet became deeply engrossed in the deal. I didn't like the look on Carter's face—a superior smirk.

A line from Hemingway's *Death in the Afternoon* ran through my head: ". . . I know only that what is moral is what you feel good after and what is immoral is what you feel bad after."

So I had to ask. "Tell me, Carter. How do you feel right now? Good?"

"Me?" He grinned. "Never felt better."

"Is nothing sacred?" I asked my wife across the table.

"Not much, old buddy," Carter answered, picking up his cards. "Not much at all."

I thought: Maybe that's why we bridge players are such an unhappy lot. Especially when we are victims of the Alcatraz Coup. I use it now, and believe me, it feels better being on the other end.

So much for morality.

2
The Way Things Are

THE FIRST STEP

The first step toward winning at bridge is to become not only suspicious and watchful of others but also to realize that for the most part, you are playing with a group of people who have the instincts of ax murderers.

Let's face it: To bridge people, *bridge is all*. Period. They will win any way they can. If you expect to win, you must be prepared to do the same. So sharpen your ax.

If I hadn't objected so vehemently to Carter Lyndhurst's failure to follow suit when he could have, and if I had thought his action was an oversight or purely unintentional—an absentminded error, so to speak (believe me, I have never been so naive)—I would not have learned about the Alcatraz Coup, which is so often and cruelly perpetrated upon the unsuspecting and the unprepared.

What is bridge, anyway? To paraphrase Arthur Koestler, the game of bridge is essentially a trial of wits played within a

The first step toward winning is to realize that for the most part, you are playing with a group of people who have the instincts of ax murderers.

matrix, which is defined by rules. Unfortunately, the very rules that should protect the innocent often militate against them and protect the guilty instead, as we have seen.

Is bridge really a sea of such scoundrels as Carter Lyndhurst? Early in my bridge-playing I found myself wondering about that. After watching Miles Evart perform, I also wondered how many of the faces that had comprised my opposition over the years were really talented cardsharps. Even if they were only half as talented as Evart, such players could neatly and unobtrusively have seeded their hands with honors and points and advantageous distribution without my knowing it.

I have, through the years, become familiar with the ways players gain edges, such as Carter Lyndhurst's use of the rules to his advantage. Some players specialize in communicating in ways that are supposed to be illegal but actually prove to be less than that in practice, as the bridge players among us have already discovered. Others are deft in the art of manipulating and intimidating. Still others are out-and-out cheats who employ ruses, diversions, bad manners, and all sorts of dirty tricks that are almost impossible to detect because they have been perfected over the years.

Sufficient Unto the Day . . .

It all comes down to this: Bridge players are a many-faceted species in whose hearts, as Lamont Cranston would say, lurks who knows how much evil. Unexorcised, they perform their devilish deeds at the bridge table (murdering the opposition), some with more savoir faire and *chutzpa* (two valuable attributes, by the way) than others.

Yes, friends, that is the truth in River City and everywhere else. If you don't believe it, go forth and watch people playing for money at rubber bridge (or the shortened version, Chicago) or vying for points at sanctioned duplicate bridge games (up from Junior Master through all the gates to Life Master, and you've won it all).

Let me tell you: *It's war!*

No army is more dedicated or more determined to annihilate the enemy than is North and South versus East and West. In time, bridge becomes an obsession, the participants narcotized. Walk through those tournament halls or visit the club car on a transcontinental or commuter train. There you will find aficionados becoming buffs, buffs turning into fanatics, and fanatics changing into zealots before your very eyes. And usually it's the zealots who beat the fanatics who beat the buffs who beat the aficionados. The aficionados beat only the uninitiated, the great bridge as yet unwashed.

Mama–Papa Bridge is the kind of bridge most of us play (or did play) because it is fun, Blackwood is bid once every two weeks with attendant great excitement (Wow! Maybe it'll go to slam!), and nobody has heard of Maltais.* What's more, nobody cares or really *wants* to know.

But to the true believer, Mama–Papa Bridge is a dirty phrase, because that kind of bridge-playing is so unsubtle, so simple. The dedicated gamester quickly graduates into the Jacoby Transfer, short clubs, Stayman, Roman Blackwood, direct cue-bids, and the negative double.

---

* The Maltais Convention is a planned variation of the Stayman Convention called the Stayman After Overcall invented by R. Maltais of Kenogami, Quebec.

Buying Master Points

In any case, as in war, to the victor go the spoils, which in the case of bridge is money (anywhere from a half cent a point to a dollar a point) at rubber bridge and status (anywhere from Junior Master to Life Master) at duplicate. And that status can be bought.

Some people pay professionals to be their partners in sanctioned tournaments in order to amass points and, therefore, achieve envied status without ever actually reaching that level of competency. The going rate of pay to play with a bridge pro like Paul Soloway of Beverly Hills for your partner, for example, is $35 a session ($70 a day) at smaller tournaments and up to $300 a day or more at the larger ones. And Soloway is no slouch. A Life Master is a bridge player who has at least 300 master points, which often take years to accumulate—but Soloway has more than 9,000 points!

On the other hand, there is underhanded bridge, and that is what many people play consciously or unconsciously (and I lean toward the consciously) because they can't afford mentors like Soloway, because they want to test their mettle (their own, their partners', and their opponents'), or because they want to earn a little money.

On the commuters' specials, for example, the flim-flammery is quite flagrant, for here one can see seconds being dealt,* and there is always a little fancy false riffling or stacking of the deck going on, most of it with a steady and comforting calculated-to-distract patter à la Miles Evart.

---

* Second dealer: A cheat who deals out the second card from a deck rather than the correct top card.

Underhanded Bridge

Nobody's Perfect

Alas—and I hate to be the bearer of such a disillusioning truth —at both rubber bridge and duplicate there often is (shame!) collusion between two or more players, as we shall see.

At a half a cent or a cent a point, a few hours' time at rubber bridge can be a pleasantly diverting and profitable pastime. At a dollar a point it can be devastating. And since, for the record, everyone seems to agree that no one cheats at bridge, who is going to complain to the police if he has been swindled at an apparently gentlemanly game of bridge either on the train (for money) or in the hallowed halls of the duplicate bridge parlors (for self-aggrandizement, or whatever)?

To say that no one cheats at bridge is to say that no one ever exceeds the speed limit. La Rochefoucauld was right: "He who lives without folly is not so wise as he thinks." To which I might add that my personal philosophy is that a successful peek is worth two or more finesses, if not game. And I have a feeling that this philosophy is shared by most bridge devotees, including the experts (who would probably deny it).

Violations at the bridge table are, according to the rules of ethics, assumed to occur either through carelessness or ignorance, which strangely does not ascribe very human motives or characteristics to the players. It is my belief that if man were not driven to deceive, mislead, and hoodwink others, the rules of bridge would not in themselves be so obsessed with the idea of improper conduct. It is right that they should be, however, for it seems that it is man's penchant to go as far as he is permitted, as long as the "proprieties" look good and properly reassuring on paper.

Nonetheless, I have often wondered if it is possible that the rules' hysterical scorn for those who would cheat and their threatened "ostracism," is merely the voicing of a dislike for those traits that every bridge player finds in himself.

THE GRAETTINGER STANCE

Take Alex Graettinger, for example. I ran into him at Laurelwood Place, one of the more important and prominent Southern California bridge clubs. He is a retired colonel and had, at the time, accumulated more than fifty master points and was an accredited National Master who looked forward to becoming a Senior Master, an Advanced Senior Master, a Life Master, and eventually—should he live so long—being elected a life member of the American Contract Bridge League.

Graettinger, who thinks he doesn't take any undue advantage in his jousts at the bridge table (but is actually one of the worst offenders in this regard that I've ever met), once responded to a remark of mine about cheating by regarding me with a jaundiced eye and then saying, "Young man, you've got it all wrong. There is no such thing as cheating. Bridge laws aren't even *designed* to prevent cheating."

"They're not?" I knew this, but his attitude irked me and I wanted to draw him out.

"Of course they're not. The laws don't even *recognize* cheating. In fact, there is no provision for redress in such a contingency, should it ever occur, God forbid." He continued rather loftily, "If you'd take the time, you would discover that the laws specifically take the view that it would be wrong to give cheats a status." Graettinger, who is a big man with a heavy black mustache, harrumphed like an old walrus and went on: "If we find a cheat here in Laurelwood Place, we'll drum him out of the corps, you can bet your bottom dollar on *that*."

"In other words, you ostracize him."

"He won't be able to find a partner anywhere, if that's what you mean." He smiled thinly. "Word gets around; don't think it doesn't." Then he added gruffly, "There *are* the proprieties, you know. And they *must* be observed. Otherwise there would be chaos. There are no penalties for intentional violations simply because they never occur. The accent's all on moral obligation, which is just where it ought to be."

Yet this same man, this Alex Graettinger, when he played that evening in a duplicate tournament, along with his partner and with malice aforethought, refused to recognize his opponents. He did not even look at them when they came to sit down to play, and neither did his partner. It was as if the new people were invisible. Being a senior member, his rudeness was one of the most intimidating performances I had ever witnessed.

To top it off, Graettinger's eyes became fish-eye cold and hard. If any question by the new couple *had* to be answered, Graettinger would turn his head slowly and disdainfully, an icy glaze to his eyes, and with the most contemptuous raspy tone of voice he could muster, would give the most vague reply possible commensurate with bare good taste and a token nod to the rules.

The proprieties, you know. Oh, you'd love Alex Graettinger. He *never* cheats. He just grinds you down slowly and exceedingly fine. Also mercilessly. But that's his thing. You see, that's the way Graettinger and his partner work. As we move along, we will observe the modus operandi of other carnivore indigenous to the terrain, some with and some without protective coloration, but all ready to move in for the kill at the first signs of weakness.

READY . . . AIM . . . FIRE!

The purpose of this book is to help you (1) identify the Graettingers, the Lyndhursts, and the other culprits among us, for you probably have been intimidated and duped many times without even knowing it; (2) to provide a means of combatting intimidators, deceivers, and would-be swindlers; and (3) to learn how to play dirty bridge yourself. And if you do, you will have plenty of company.

You'd better believe it.

3
Establishing Superiority

Clarence A. Hibbing is a chubby Glendale bachelor who often throws his home open to games. When he is not having tables, he's making a fourth at bridge somewhere else, either at rubber or duplicate. He is a rather carefree, likable fellow given to far-out puns and wry jokes. He is also a below-average bridge player who wins far more games (and rubber bridge money) than he should.

How does he do it? Simple. He always makes sure he never plays with opponents who have not been to his home, for in the entrance hall, where guests are certain not to miss it, stands a gigantic display case. Inside it are all his bridge trophies.

The case is French provincial, a beautifully handcrafted, solid walnut, lighted cabinet with cabriole legs, three glass sides, and two sliding doors (always locked). It stands eight feet high and is six feet wide. Inside, on the various shelves, are the highly polished, gleaming trophies—some gold, some silver—all suitably inscribed with Clarence Hibbing's name and the names of tournaments and the places where they were played.

Hibbing is very modest about his prizes. When someone mentions them (usually in a voice edged with awe and veneration), Hibbing is apt to shrug and say, as if embarrassed, "Oh, them . . ." He will then change the subject. Questioners are usually put off by this show of humility and will not pursue it in deference to Hibbing's obvious bashful feelings.

The truth of the matter is that *Hibbing has never won a trophy in his life!* What's more, Hibbing never actually *says* he has won those trophies. He just lets his guests see them and draw their own conclusions. And their conclusion usually is: "How can we expect to win against a man who has won the Tuplifsky Trophy three times running, the Corn Belt Regional, and was a member of the knockout team of the Middling Sectional last year? Especially when the Corn Belt Regional trophy is nearly five feet high topped by a silvery wood nymph offering a wreath of corncobs in arms stretched heavenward?"

First-time guests are usually so discomposed at the sight of all this that they find their tongues sticking to the roofs of their mouths, they bid all wrong, and they simply can't keep track of the cards. All they can see is those trophies. And if they had agreed to come to Hibbing's place for a cent-a-point night, they are sure to go home heavy losers.

After the games Hibbing can usually be found shining, waxing, and polishing the goodies in the trophy case he never unlocks for anybody, humming wicked little tunes as he does so. He's got a good thing going and has always been careful to use dates and places that sound legitimate. As he rubs the gleaming metal, he reflects on how easy it is to let other people's erroneous assumptions win games for him.

Underhanded Bridge

BLACKWOOD'S DAZZLING INVENTION

Is this cheating? In my opinion, if it weren't for Clarence Hibbing and other such dissemblers, the bridge world would be a much more bland place than it is, for the laws of contract and duplicate have become so full of checks and balances that if players were not always inventing new ways to deceive their opponents, it would hardly be the challenging game it is.

Systems of fraud and deception (new card conventions, doubles, and transfers) start out as blatant tricks but in time, through use and widespread adoption by other players, become accepted or, to coin a word, "conventional." Those who do not catch on quickly enough lose out.

Can you imagine what happened that fateful day in 1933 when twenty-year-old Easley Blackwood (let's say he's South and bidding spades) first uttered his famous words, "Four no trump," and started what has become the Blackwood Convention? North had to be in on it, of course. But think of the looks East and West must have exchanged!

Let us fantasize further:

"Double," West says. He and his partner have been bidding diamonds and there is simply no way his right hand opponent (RHO), Blackwood, is going to make four no trump.

North responds, "Five diamonds."

East must have gasped at this. Why, this is the very suit he and West have been bidding! How can North/South do this? He (East) has the ace and more than a good share of diamonds, and his partner has indicated he's got the rest of the diamonds. Have Blackwood and his friend North gone completely out of their minds?

"Double!" East says heartily.

"Five no trump," Blackwood declares.

"Double!" West says. Oh, this is going to be easy, West thinks. North and South are going to be set and set good. And they're vulnerable, too.

"Six hearts," North says.

East can believe neither his eyes nor his ears. Why, in addition to the diamonds, he's got four hearts headed by the king! "Double!" he shouts, exultant.

And then Blackwood quietly bids his six spades, which he could not have done had he not found out what he wanted to know: precisely how many aces and kings his partner has.

"Double!" screams West.

"Redouble," North says calmly.

East and West probably did not appreciate until years later how they were so cleverly hoodwinked by an inventive young man named Blackwood who went on in that game to win twelve tricks, crossruffing and rendering East's diamonds worthless.

THE NAME OF THE GAME

Take falsecarding, for another example. Think of the defender who first decided to play a card other than his lowest with the intention of deceiving the declarer, which he probably did. So he did it again. And again. Now it is such a common fraud that defenders are forced to vary their signals between "true" and "false" cards to persuade the declarer to ruff unnecessarily or perhaps ruff high in critical trump situations.

Or consider still another example. Suppose you and your partner have clubs, hearts, and diamonds. It follows then that your opponents are going to have all or most of the spades, in which case it also follows that, in the auction, a bid of spades by *you* (weak in spades as you are) is going to inhibit *their* lead play in spades (even though they may try to convince themselves it's preemptory), especially if one of your strong minors is not even mentioned in the bidding. Your opponent then might be deceived into leading right into your strength—which helps if you're vulnerable, doubled, and you've redoubled (you have, haven't you?), or helps even if you have nothing on, or just a partial.

Who says bridge isn't a game of traps and deceits? If Clarence Hibbing wants to extend it off the table (and much of the game is off the table), who can blame him?

Then there are what were once "artificial" bids. They were invented to deceive the enemy through agreement between partners about their meaning, and they are now commonplace. I refer to takeout doubles; "bust" responses of two no trump to opening two bids; the so-called cipher bids, which have nothing to do with the suit indicated (or any other suit, for that matter); the Stayman responses; and the now conventional two club opener with a blockbuster hand; and trap passing.

Times change, however. Blackwood's day is past. Now you must "alert" the opposition when you're trying out some new kind of bid, which is to say you're making an attempt to communicate with your partner in a way that might confuse your opposition. Already they're reaching for your convention card. "Let's not try to pull something," they're saying, if you haven't alerted them in the proper manner.

The chances for deception are therefore becoming more limited every day, which leads us to the next question: Is there nothing left for the resourceful, imaginative player who is willing to take a few risks?

THE GENTLE ART OF BULLDOZING

Well, there's always Clarence Hibbing, as I've said. But we can't all be Hibbings. There must be other ways of establishing superiority or creating an aura of invincibility besides running out to buy trophies and having them engraved to yourself. There are other ways, and they're cheaper, too. All it takes is a little browbeating, bullying, and intimidating, all perfectly legal and performed (preferably) before the first card is dealt.

I call the process bulldozing, though that is a rather harsh word for what is really the art of being an amiable poseur. Let me give you an example.

There's a fellow I know named Norman Pachuta who is an expert at a little routine that is enormously effective at either duplicate or rubber bridge (for money). Norman sits down with a big smile and begins at once to make a search through his pockets for a match or a pencil or a handkerchief—anything that will give him the chance to spill out on the table a pocketful of pink slips signed by tournament directors.

"Sorry," Norman will say before anyone has a chance to help him gather them up and, in the process, perhaps find out they're not real. "I've got so many of these darn winning things I'm ashamed to turn them in. Never had such a streak of luck before in my life!"

It is very disquieting. A pall of resignation and gloom seems to settle over the table as the cheerful Norman rubs his hands together and says, "Well, shall we get started?"

OTHER DISCOURAGEMENTS

Perhaps by this time you are beginning to understand that the attitude engendered in the opposition—hopefully that of resignation or despair—is worth more than high cards or fancy bidding. Eliciting such feelings in the enemy and the resultant despondent bidding, bad plays, and blunders are matters of posture—*your* posture. This does not mean being something you're not; it means being as inventive as possible—peripherally. Assuming for the moment there is nothing you can do about the cards and that your bidding and play is at least average, there are other areas that could use your attention. To wit:

Before the game is started, you ought to make offhand and easy reference to obscure or nonexistent conventions, such as, "You *do* play the Herbert Negative, I presume," which would be obscure, or "Does anyone mind if I (or we) play Simonson?" which was the name of your grandfather on your mother's side (and he *never* played bridge), both remarks being infuriatingly intimidating. Already the opposition is down one.

At the very least these seemingly innocent questions will force your opponent(s) to ask what each is or suffer the embarrassment of tacitly agreeing to play the named convention without knowing what it is or when (and if) it is (or will be) used, unless you must "alert" in duplicate, in which case you may do so via a nonexistent system, which you can always claim is a psychic bid.

"I thought you knew that's what Simonson was! For heaven's sake, why didn't you ask?"

Discouraging? Yes, indeed. For *them*. They have no idea where they stand, how to proceed, or what you're going to do next. Unpredictability is a valuable asset to any bridge player, pair, or team.

Then there is the matter of referring to the great or the near-great in the game and your experiences with him or them, all of it a glorious name-dropping fabrication and terribly upsetting to the other side. This allows you to be as imaginative and colorful as you like. The game being what it is, someone may zero in or pick up on your reference, so it would be well to pick someone who has expired. For example, there is Emeric Alpar (1905–1956) of Budapest, a stockbroker and, until his death, a resident of London.

Alpar, European Champion in 1934, won the Master Pairs in Great Britain in 1946. You can always invent a story about how Alpar came to the United States (to see your father if the age thing gets in the way), and you can weave an even wilder tale out of some fancied experience—about some wild hand you (or your father) and he played in Fort Wayne, Indiana, just after the wars.

Or you can put the opposition further down when they pursue it by saying coldly, "I take it you didn't know Emeric and that you take issue with the way he played and all his inventive systems. Well, all I have to say is, at least he tried."

The mythology already surrounding bridge makes it insulting that in the ladies-and-gentlemen polite game that bridge is, one's word should be questioned, particularly when one is speaking of the dead, and especially with respect to a person who just happens to be one of bridge's greats.

If you want to thrust in further, you might add, "Are you sure you really enjoy bridge? Or is it the people who worked out the kinks and perfected the game for you that upset you?"

This is not exactly the way to make friends, but if this bothers you, then you must face the moment of truth: Why are you playing the game?

If you are playing the game to make friends, I don't know what to tell you. If you are playing bridge to win, then continue on to the next chapter.

4
Polishing Your Arrogance

THE MAN FROM MENSA

The first time I saw Harvey Ingalls, he was slipping into the chair to my left (West) with easy aplomb at a duplicate contest at the Humboldt Bridge Club in North Hollywood. He was all teeth, freckles, and fat, and he gave a hearty hello to Marty Moriches, his partner-to-be, extending a big hand and saying, "The name's Harvey Ingalls" and exposing even more teeth.

"Marty," Marty said, taking the hand. "Marty Moriches." Marty introduced me and Lloyd Kersey (North), my partner. We'd been waiting for Ingalls to make the fourth and had been engaged in small talk. We'd been a little put out at being held up.

"Don't I know you?" Ingalls asked, staring at Marty. "Wasn't it at the last Mensa meeting at the Alexander?"

"Mensa?" Marty tried to smile. "Not me. I don't belong to Mensa."

Underhanded Bridge

"Oh," Ingalls said, instantly relegating Marty to some sort of submarginal existence.

Now everybody knows that the requirements for membership in Mensa consist of but one thing: You must have an IQ higher than that of 98 percent of the rest of the world.

Ingalls' rudeness irritated me, but Lloyd beat me to a response by saying, "Oh, you're one of those, eh?"

"One of what?" Ingalls challenged. His voice had an edge of undisputable supremacy.

"What's your IQ?" I asked, trying to think of some way to puncture his ego.

"Sorry," Ingalls replied. "Can't tell you that."

"One would hardly believe it could be over a hundred," Lloyd said nastily. Ingalls was getting to him, too.

"It's high enough," Ingalls said loftily, taking his cards from the duplicate board and arranging them in his hand. "What is tragic is that some of us have nothing in common but our intelligence." He looked around the room as if trying to find someone more compatible. "A knife that only cuts butter gets frightfully dull."

We felt sorry for Marty Moriches, whom we both knew well, but we would annihilate Harvey Ingalls—yes, we would. By mutual tacit consent Lloyd Kersey and I would thrash him soundly, teach him a lesson, and apologize later to Marty for it, knowing he would understand.

So we proceeded to take Ingalls apart. We overbid, Ingalls doubled, and Lloyd redoubled the ridiculous five heart contract we found ourselves in. But Ingalls' insufferable superiority had ruined Lloyd Kersey and me. He'd made us mad. We'd lost our cool. We didn't even make our book.

Polishing Your Arrogance

Not a Popularity Contest

Later, Lloyd and I picked up the pieces and tried to find the lesson in what had happened. There was no doubt that Ingalls was a fair bridge player, probably no better than any of us. We decided that what we had done was to play right into his hands, letting him get to us with his obtrusive self-assurance and self-proclaimed preeminence.

Much later, when we got to know him, we found out that Harvey Ingalls didn't even belong to Mensa. In fact, as he reminded us, *he never actually said he did.* He told us he'd had the Mensa routine pulled on him and a partner in a tournament in Cincinnati. He finds that when he's new in a crowd it wins games and master points, at least at first.

And so it is that arrogance can replace or, at the very least, support strength in a game. It has value in bridge, which unlike chess and other games such as craps and roulette, has so many secrets and where so much of what is going on is hidden.

Look at it this way: Good players don't have to be logical or even likable; they need only be sure of themselves. If a player can convince others he knows more than they do about what is going on, his opponents will often assume that he has considered all the complicated and secret details that they find so difficult to understand, and they will not try too hard to win against him because it appears to be a lost cause.

Arrogance assumes that all the unknowns have been discovered and have been dealt with, that there are no mysteries left. And that is discouraging to players like you and me because we're not that sure of ourselves.

We see our thirteen cards. We try to work out in our minds

what we're going to do with them. Then there is the bidding. What is everyone *really* saying? Can I trust my partner? Does *he* know what he's doing? Then it comes down to your hand and the dummy's, leaving two unseen hands to worry about—a total of twenty-six cards. So many uncertainties! What to do? Inevitably, you try to bluff it out, project a confident image.

Bridge players, like most people, do not seem to hate villains and wickedness, only weakness. And that's where players like Ingalls get to them: They capitalize on the dislike of the braggart which they know is compensation for feelings of inferiority. The Ingallses of this world have something going for them: a finely honed sense of when to use arrogance.

Being unsure of ourselves, we can often spot uncertainty in others. "Well, at least I don't have to worry about East," we say, if East is chewing his lower lip in agonizing indecisiveness. But we are apt to give up in the face of strength or overreact in the face of arrogance.

It doesn't take much to appear formidable, just use a touch of arrogance, a look of the bridge fanatic (practice this in the mirror), be able to make a serious statement about the game, and project the approach of a winning, no-nonsense competitive spirit. Strive for flair, daring, and use a lot of imagination.

FIGHTING BLUSTER AND SHOW

Suppose you are being encroached upon by blowhards and intimidators. What should you do? The best thing is to fight fire with fire. One way is to use nostalgia.

Refer to Dwight D. Eisenhower and your experiences with him in the army (or afterward, for that matter), and recall the general's bridge game with Mark Clark, A. M. Gruenther, and naval aide Harry C. Butcher in Gibraltar on November 7, 1942, the day of the first Allied invasion after the fall of France.

"Damn good player, Ike was," you say, shaking your head. "You really ought to read what Jacoby has to say about him."

If you are too young to have known Ike, you can always have an uncle who taught Ike all he knew, and of course your uncle, who passed on to that great duplicate tournament in the sky last year, taught *you* all *you* know.

Or, if somebody starts giving you a hard time, tell him, "You know, I've discovered a sad thing: Winners are more lonely than losers." You shake your head despairingly. A misting of the eyes will help. "They say nothing succeeds like success, but they're wrong. Since I win so often nobody speaks to me anymore." Then, with resolution: "I've got a good mind to forget points, forget the game, just make average plays, be accepted like a regular player again."

Should you be placed at the same table with a couple you've been told is going to be difficult, then introduce the partner you've brought with you as if everybody ought to know him (or her), implying that your partner is a "name" in the bridge world, a lesser name, perhaps, but a name to be sure, one in the ascendancy, and your opposition's ignorance will show when they can't place him.

You might even lie about your partner's master points. After all, you could have misunderstood what he said he had. Make it a large number. Your partner can always counter with, "Oh, come now, I'm not that good. I don't have that many."

This opposition-frightening modesty ploy (it is frightening because such modesty is unheard of in bridge circles and for that reason it is also ominous) will work even if your partner has no master points, and it is guaranteed to simmer up there in your opponents' brains all during the match, helping to muddy up their bidding and play.

Your Accomplice Partner

There are many excellent scripts that can be written to display needful arrogance if your partner is a willing participant. Such maneuvers are useful against opponents who are coming on strong or who would try to impress you with their own mastery of every facet of the bridge scene. Here is an example:

YOU: Is it *la longue d'abord* ("long suit first") *sans atout* ("in no trump")?

PARTNER: The *tendance canapé* ("canapé tendency") is to bid minimum hands in normal fashion but use the principle for hands of good strength.

YOU: Thank you, partner. The reason I asked is I've always found Albarran's rule confusing.

PARTNER: Just think of it as the long suit on the second round, not with a two-suited hand of more than minimum strength bidding the higher-ranking suit first if it has four cards and on the second if it has more than four.

YOU: Thanks for clearing that up.

PARTNER: Actually, I never bid a canapé.

YOU: Why not?

PARTNER: It always makes me hungry.

YOU: Let's order a pizza.

PARTNER: I'd rather bid it than eat it.

YOU: *Sans atout?*

PARTNER: *A outrance* ("to the death").

YOU: *A peu de frais* ("at little expense")?

PARTNER: *A point* ("exactly")!

And another:

YOU: When does *a priori* become *a posteriori?*

PARTNER: After the cards have been seen.

YOU: What about probabilities *a posteriori?*

PARTNER: The *a priori* probability of an initial split against an even division is exactly the same as the ratio between the *a posteriori* probabilities.

YOU: That makes sense.

PARTNER: Probabilities *a priori* are the basic probabilities of a given distribution of cards expressed as a fraction where the numerator is the total number of favorable cases and the denominator the total number of equally likely possible cases.

YOU: In other words, it's like an inference that leaves no room for doubt and is therefore a deduction. I've always felt, over the long haul, that the cards and their values even out, so expert play is necessary in order to win. Do you believe that?

PARTNER: Yes. Lesser players merely play on while those with skill and mathematical deliberation make points.

YOU: Do you mean that there is probably a high correlation between the ability to learn the elements of bridge and mathematical aptitude and a rather lower correlation with intelligence quotient?

PARTNER: Look around you, partner.

YOU: [*With a sigh*] Yes, I see what you mean.

And one last example:

YOU: Partner, do you ever feel guilty when you hold face cards?

PARTNER: You mean the Devil's Tickets?

YOU: I see you're familiar with the concept of graven images and how the Puritans felt it was a violation of the second commandment.

PARTNER: Am I ever! But don't forget that in 1397 John I, King of Castile, forbade dice and cards. I wonder if he died of his excesses.

YOU: I wouldn't know. I do know that in 1897 the Provost of Paris forbade playing at dice or cards on workdays.

PARTNER: Amazing that you should mention it, for it only reminds me that in 1423 St. Bernardin persuaded the people of Bologna to throw their cards into the fire.

YOU: Ah, yes. And because it was thought to be a waste of time, playing at cards was forbidden by the Parliament of Paris in 1541. Maybe it *is* a waste of time. Ever think of that?

PARTNER: It depends upon one's opponents, wouldn't you say?

YOU: Without a doubt. [*Pause*] Present company excepted, of course.

PARTNER: (*After a cough*] Of course.

Helpful Little Irritants

I don't know why it is, but bridge people who possess oddments of bridge arcana are able to make their opponents suffer through some sense of inferiority when these are cited. It is as if they say to themselves, "If he knows this, how much more does he know than I?"

"Interesting" facts that you want to "share" with the table (hopefully, with your partner's permission) can prove to be irritants that cloud the opposition's bidding, throw them off-stride, and make them play erratically. Yet you can't be faulted. After all, you are *offering* something. Often it gives you more depth and makes them think you are more resourceful than you really are. Here are some examples that can be brought to the table's attention at the right moments:

—A player can have five spades in 79,181,063,676 ways.

—Write 66,905,856,160/635,013,559,600 on a piece of paper, show it to everyone, and then say, "Before the cards are seen, the probability that a particular player will hold a 4–3–3–3 hand pattern is precisely this figure. Interesting, don't you think?" (Don't expect to be applauded.)

—The earliest use of cards for play (and also for money) was in China in 969 A.D. The deck had four suits of 14 cards each.

—Tell them that the number of possible deals is 53,644,737,-765,488,792,839,237,440,000. Then tell them how interesting that is and ask for comments. Discount the unprintable expletives as overreaction or envy formation. Sometimes the comments are more interesting than the offered facts, especially if you are not a sensitive person. The least it will do is tell you something about the players (and the human race).

—A *coup en blanc* is a ducking play for the purpose of winning a later trick.

—There are 39 possible hand patterns 4-3-3-3 to 13-0-0-0, and a player can hold four spades, three hearts, three diamonds and three clubs in 13C4x13C3x13C3x13C3 different ways, the C standing for *cards*, which (you tell them) computes to 16,726,464,040, or 2.634 percent of the 635,013,559,600 hands. If they are not interested, it may be they have no head for figures.

—Your chance of getting a Yarborough (hands with all cards lower than nine) are 1,827 to 1.

—An assumption that a violation by an opponent is

intentional is as much a violation of ethics as would be such an intentional violation itself, don't you think? If you get blank stares, at least you are getting *something*.

If anybody objects to what you are doing, say, "I can see you're a book player. Let me ask you, do you know what A. W. Drayton said about book players? He said, 'The book player is a safe partner but is not very dangerous as an adversary.' "

That will shut them up. Don't let anything discourage your pursuit of and willingness to share these valuable bits and pieces about your (and their) game.

5
Psyching Out the Opposition

The Value of Suggestion

I was playing unusually well, making every bid, successfully blocking my opponents, and making no errors in reading my partner. Then Marsha, who was playing East this rubber bridge night, had to go and say, "You know, schizophrenics often have a period just before their illnesses when they have ESP to an extraordinary degree and everything seems to go right for them. Unusally right." She was looking at me meaningfully and she was wearing the faintest of smiles.

From then on things went badly for me. I didn't make a single bid. I played like a different person. Nothing seemed to work out.

I knew what it was: Marsha had gotten to me. I kept thinking about what she'd said. Why, indeed, was I playing so well? Way over my head. Of course Marsha was (and still is) Dr. Marsha Brantley, psychiatrist, but I don't think it would have mattered

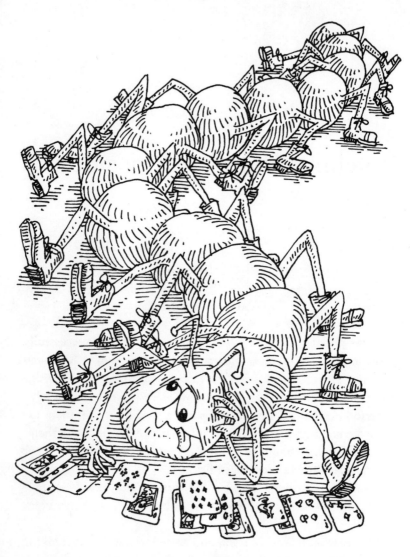

Marsha had gotten to me. What she'd done was to get me thinking about myself like the centipede thinking about its feet. And as I was thinking about it, the magic disappeared.

what or who she was. What she'd done was to get me thinking about myself, like the centipede thinking about his feet. How was I doing what I was doing? What was I doing right? And as I was thinking about it, the magic disappeared.

Marsha laughed about it later when I told her she'd ruined my game. "You're very suggestible," she said. "But then everybody is. Didn't you know that?"

I told her I hadn't thought much about it.

"Oh, and it's true about schizophrenics, in case you were wondering."

"Witch doctor," I hissed, half-meaning it.

"Oh, come on, all's fair in bridge and war."

"I thought that was 'love and war.' "

Marsha shrugged. "Lovers, bridge players, and generals all expect to win their little games. Another thing: Nobody ever really practices at winning at love, bridge, or war. People want—and expect—to win right from the start, and when they don't, they're likely to put the blame somewhere else. 'Nothing but bad hands,' one woman will say. 'Bad distribution killed me.' Or 'For everybody else finesses work at least half the time, but for me . . . well, you were here, you saw.' You know the type: excuses, excuses."

I was still miffed by her clever maneuver. "There's no charge for this little lecture, I hope."

"Don't knock it," Marsha said. "Build up an arsenal of tricks yourself."

I sighed. "I honestly don't know why I play this game, Marsha. I really don't."

"Shall I tell you?" It would have been impolite to try to stop her. "It's because you want to prove something either to yourself or to other people. Bridge players are like gamblers. They're only alive when their fate rests on the turn of a card or when they are moving in for the kill. Life beyond that simply does not exist for them in much of any degree of what the rest of us know as reality."

That seemed a bit harsh, but I admitted I'd seen players like that. "Also race drivers, sky divers, and combat infantrymen," I added.

Marsha nodded. "Now you've got it. 'If Fate likes me, I'll survive.' They mean 'win.' That's their thinking. Sometimes I think all they want to do is show they are superior to others, sometimes even to life itself."

"How about you, Marsha?"

Her smile was teasing. "Why else would I be here?"

I didn't know how to take her. Psychiatrists are a strange breed. But I've thought a lot about it since, and it seems to me, driven the way they are, and with that great expectation of winning pushing them, bridge players render themselves susceptible to some of the most outrageous psychological trickery imaginable, which was what Marsha was implying.

I think this is because beneath the surface, as I've said, players aren't really all that sure of themselves. With some, their insecurities are worn like Rotarian badges over their hearts. With others it is buried as deep within them as their livers. But just remember: It's there, even if you can't see it. They may behave like God's gifts to the bridge world, superior to you and the game, overbearing and important, but it's quite likely they're overcompensating.

In any event, whether their unsureness is large or small or even nonexistent, it behooves us—whether these players are kith or kin, lodge, blood, or soul brothers—to defang them early, dull their scythes, blunt their weapons, defuse their bombs, and deflate their ridiculous egos.

So, if you and your partner are North and South, there is no reason under the sun why you shouldn't alter reality a little for East and West. If they're winning, tell them about schizos. If you think they might try a quick clobber, beat them to it with a little psychological warfare.

MORVIN THE SEED-SOWER

A fellow I know named Leonard Morvin has a routine that works for him more times than not, mostly because it engenders vague but frightening doubts in the mind of an opponent. He waits until he can speak to one of his adversaries alone, first determining that neither knows the other very well, although this is not crucial. This can be done at the water cooler, the coffee table, kitchen, hallway, or even at the table itself.

MORVIN: How come you're playing with Hulbert?

OPPONENT: Why do you ask?

MORVIN: How well do you know him?

OPPONENT: Hulbert? Oh, I've played with him a few times. I still don't see——

MORVIN: Then you don't know him very well.

OPPONENT: I guess you could say that. But you still haven't told me why you——

MORVIN: Well . . . since you don't know him, and it's easy to see that you don't . . . Oh, I don't think I'd better say.

OPPONENT: Say what?

MORVIN: Well, it's pretty well-known that he . . . [*now abashedly*] look, I'm sorry I brought it up. Forget I even started this conversation, will you?

OPPONENT: It must be important if you——

MORVIN: I could cut off my tongue. I really could, and I'm sorry. It just wouldn't be fair to you, to Hulbert, or to me to mention it. I'm afraid I'm going to have to beg your indulgence about this.

OPPONENT: Well, all right. But I still think——

MORVIN: Thank you. I feel better now.

Without saying a single detrimental thing about Hulbert—or anything at all, for that matter—Morvin has succeeded in making Hulbert's partner queasy about Hulbert and has probably damaged their game. If Hulbert's partner mentions this little episode to Hulbert, and this seldom happens, and Morvin is confronted, Morvin is affronted.

MORVIN: What do you mean, what bad thing do I know about you?

HULBERT: What you were going to tell my partner here. If you were going to say it, I've got a right to know what it is.

MORVIN: It was a mistake, Hulbert, believe me. I could see that when I started to say it. So I didn't go on.

HULBERT: Say what? What do you know about me? You're making me mad, you know, going around talking behind my back. I think you'd better start explaining.

MORVIN:[*With a sigh*] All right. If that's the way you feel about it, I'll explain. I was going to tell him what a good guy you were and what a great bridge player you are. That's all. Then I saw that saying that would only be aiding and comforting the enemy, so I shut up. That's all there is to it. Honest.

HULBERT: [*He has to be reeling*] Oh . . . well, gosh, Leonard, I . . . I didn't realize . . . I——

MORVIN: [*Walking away*] Forget it.

As Morvin walks away, hiding his smirk, Hulbert has already forgotten that he and his partner lost the night's game because of Morvin.

Variations on a Scheme

Leonard Morvin has a variation on this routine that involves a partner. It goes something like this:

Sometime during the game, preferably early, or even before the game starts, he covertly asks to see one of his opponents privately; he has something to tell him. We'll say the opponent he talks to is East.

Morvin says that what he has to say is confidential, that his (Morvin's) partner is out on parole and he (Morvin) thought it best to say something about it.

"Johnson"—Morvin's partner—"is a nice guy, really," Morvin says. Then he shakes his head. "Can't see him doing it, that's all."

Naturally, East wants to know more, so Morvin, with great reluctance, gives it to him piece by piece, beginning with how he served six years for murder. "It was, actually, only a third of his sentence." Then the fact that the victim was his wife comes out. "You never saw much about it in the paper," Morvin goes on. "It was hushed up. But it was a case very similar to the Bennett murder, you know, the one after the bridge game. It was made famous by Wollcott in *While Rome Burns*. A true case, by the way."

Then, pulling on the lobe of his ear and looking around to make sure his partner isn't listening, Morvin continues, "I just wanted to say that if Johnson acts strange in any way, just remember he's been dummying up in a penitentiary for years, so don't think anything of it."

East usually doesn't know what to say.

Morvin says, "Of course if Johnson gets violent, I'll need help. Okay?"

East swallows, nods, and they go back to the table where East gets West aside to tell him about Johnson at the first opportunity. Their play goes (predictably) downhill after this startling revelation.

Morvin has worked out other variations to fit the mood, temper, and progress of the game. Sometimes his partner is out on bail from a mad bomber charge. "You know, those people that were killed over at Randolph in front of the post office," Morvin says. Or he's got Johnson accused of multiple murders. "But anybody can see Johnson wouldn't go berserk. He's an Eagle Scout and teaches Sunday School at the Presbyterian Church. Just because he has these spells . . ." Morvin's voice trails off and he never elaborates. Imagination unbridled is a wonderful weapon once you've set it in motion, as Morvin knows.

6
How to Set Up Roadblocks and Detours

Calvin Jewett and Larry Dunstable are partners in an architectural business that takes them all over the country. They are also inveterate bridge players, the kind that bridge expert and columnist Alfred Sheinwold was talking about when he said in the March 25, 1974, issue of the Los Angeles *Times*, "A great bridge player, if asked to choose between a night of bridge and a date with a sex symbol . . . would unhesitatingly play bridge. A girl is a girl. A bridge game is a challenge beyond compare."

If Jewett and Dunstable were to fail as architects, it would not be half the tragedy it would be if they were to fail as bridge players. As it is, with three American Contract Bridge League Nationals, 63 Regionals, and 645 Sectional tournaments to go to annually (reservations for hotel space for bridge players are greater than reservations for all other American activities!),

Jewett and Dunstable are hard pressed to find time to be architects.

Having played for years, Jewett and Dunstable have learned the ins and outs of bridge-table infighting—both the practical and psychological aspects of it. Early in their tournament play they discovered that a continuous line of dialogue (before play) is helpful and can prove to be unnerving to the opposition. This works equally well in either tournament or stakes play, though the subject matter and the degree to which it can be used varies with the circumstances.

In sanctioned play there are the proprieties, and the director stands nearby ready to be summoned by the opposition at the slightest irregularity (to say nothing of the screens now in use in final play), so the verbal exchanges are limited to pregame or between-game periods. In rubber bridge for money there is more latitude, and the approach is more casual, though it is often more deadly, as we shall see.

The key to this winning combination is that when Jewett and Dunstable are evenly matched or they know the opposition has a better track record than they have, they try to discover their antagonists' Achilles' heels. Is it politics? Religion? Business?

Let us assume that Jewett and Dunstable are North/South and that East/West are reserved and refined. If that is the case, then North's and South's winning posture is that of being perfect boors. This will cause East/West to come off their game. It is a matter of being able to play off each other like actors or comedians. Here is an example:

At a sectional tournament Jewett and Dunstable had to play the Cutshins—Alex and Mae—who were odds-on favorites to place somewhere in the very top positions. North/South (Jewett/Dunstable) discovered that the Cutshins were extremely conservative politically, though they were quite liberal and daring in their bidding and play. So North/South found little difficulty improvising a routine calculated to disturb the Cutshins, capitalizing on their strong feelings and, in the process, ruining their tournament play at a crucial time, thereby aiding their own. The exchange went something like this:

JEWETT: You know, Larry, these Communists are clever. You can't help but admire them.

DUNSTABLE: Why do you say that, Cal?

JEWETT: Well, look at us. Here we are in the United States of America and we're playing a Russian game.

DUNSTABLE: [*Outraged*] A Russian game!

JEWETT: Sure. Didn't you know the Commies invented bridge?

DUNSTABLE: I don't believe it!

JEWETT: It's true. The earliest mention of the game of bridge appeared in a Russian pamphlet in 1886, and that was long after Marxism got its start there. [*After a laugh*] Who knows, maybe Karl Marx himself invented the game. I know Trotsky was said to be a good player.

DUNSTABLE: Now wait a minute, Cal——

JEWETT: The pamphlet was entitled *Biritch or Russian Whist.* That's where the word *bridge* originated.

DUNSTABLE: Isn't there anything these Russians didn't invent?

JEWETT: We know they invented bridge because Biritch resembles Vint, Preference, and other Russian card games.

DUNSTABLE: Do you think we're unpatriotic, playing bridge the way we do?

JEWETT: I've often thought about that. It's a wonder the game never got investigated by the House Un-American Activities Committee. [*Looking around*] I wonder . . . how many Commies do you suppose are playing here tonight?

Now the Cutshins could have ignored the dialogue—they should have kept their cool—but they didn't. They quickly reached critical mass and, following an explosive exchange (all of the exploding being on the Cutshins' side), the Cutshins failed miserably in this and ensuing games.

At a regional tourney Jim and Alice Franklin, a couple Jewett and Dunstable had heard of, were to be their opposition along the way. Now the Franklins were formidable opponents; it was going to take some doing to defeat them. So our North/South partners used what they knew about the Franklins to get to them. The secret was that the Franklins were quite proper, particulary Mrs. Franklin, who was a big contributor to "decency" groups. So Calvin Jewett let fly with this little gem:

JEWETT: Larry, I want you to know I've always admired your blue peter.

MRS. FRANKLIN [*Shocked*] I beg your pardon!

DUNSTABLE: Oh, it's true, Mrs. Franklin. And I really know how to use it, too. Of course it's taken practice—and practice makes perfect, you know.

MR. FRANKLIN: See here now, you two——

JEWETT: Too bad neither of you is familiar with it. [*With a blush*] Use it sometimes myself . . .

MRS. FRANKLIN: [*Mortified*] Oh!

JEWETT: But I'm not as good as Larry is with it.

Just before the Franklins looked as if they were ready to blow their tops, Jewett and Dunstable "suddenly" tumbled to what the Franklins were thinking, so they explained that "blue peter" isn't a scatological term, that it's an entirely proper term for a high–low bridge signal and was invented in 1834 by Lord Henry Bentinck—weren't they aware of that?

They elaborated, telling the Franklins that the term is nautical in origin and refers to a signal that is hoisted in the harbor to show when a ship is ready to sail out to sea. They apologized if they had offended the Franklins, but they have never themselves ever thought of blue peter except in bridge and nautical terms, repeating the words as many times as possible, and the Franklins, first offended and then not really appeased, were by this time completely derailed. They tried desperately to get back on the track, but their advantage had passed.

Outwitting the Sharpies

When Jewett and Dunstable aren't playing in sanctioned tournaments, they are usually traveling, and when they are, they always try to find partners for a bridge game. They are fond of running into couples who want to play for high stakes, because they have found that strangers eager to play for big money usually have in mind unorthodox methods of winning. When that happens, Jewett and Dunstable start one of their carefully rehearsed routines.

Dunstable (North) excuses himself the first time he is dummy (to go for coffee or a snack or whatever), and before Jewett starts to play the hand, he asks East and West whether or not they think North is holding up well.

East/West naturally want to know what he means by that, so Jewett says, "What I mean is . . ." He has difficulty going on, tries again: "I mean, all things considered . . ." He stops. Then, as if finally overcoming his reluctance to talk about it, he blurts out: "I might as well say it: This is Larry's first trip on the outside."

"The outside?" East or West will ask (usually tightening up visibly).

"Yes," Jewett says. "You see, he's going to have to face reality soon enough, which means understanding that people know what he is." Of course East/West want to know what *that* is, so Jewett tells them about Dunstable's maniacal actions, hallucinations, and delusions before he was committed to the state facility.

Then Jewett leans back, beaming. He's snared them now and he knows it. "But they've done a marvelous job on him, don't you think?"

East/West usually swallow, and not wanting to say anything else, hastily agree that "they" have, indeed, done a fine job on North. At this point they are usually wondering how they ever got into this dollar-a-point game.

Then Jewett pulls the plug. "I only wish he hadn't insisted on buying that knife," he says worriedly. "I can't understand what he expects to *do* with it."

If, later on, the already unsettled strangers look as if they might make an important game, Dunstable brings out the knife he carries and begins to pare his fingernails. It never fails to send the opposition off in the wrong (losing) direction to escape the hideous dead end they visualize might be just up ahead if they try to win.

The Bust Response Caper

When Calvin Jewett finds that Larry Dunstable is unable to accompany him on a business conference halfway across the country, Jewett takes along his cute, young, and well-endowed wife. The former Mary Fowler, for all her beauty and God-given assets, is no slouch at bridge. In fact, Jewett met her at a duplicate tournament, couldn't take his eyes off her, and asked her to marry him when, as his random partner, she helped his dazzlement flower into love by bidding him into and making a grand slam in spades doubled, redoubled, and vulnerable.

Calvin and Mary Jewett are always on the lookout for a game. Unfortunately, they often run into some shady players who let them win a rubber or two and then suggest that they play for ever-increasing stakes. At some point thereafter they put their trickery into operation.

Calvin and Mary are more than equal to such chicanery; Mary has the wardrobe for it and Calvin the lines. When they are sure they are being rooked, they maneuver the opposition into a delayed game that will decide the match.

When the four get together again, Mary has changed into her "uniform" for the final game, which is simply an eyelet blouse and skirt in matching color, plus suitable undergarments. Her attire is not in the least daring, and Mary is demure.

As the bidding starts, however, Mary brings out a hankie and begins to dab at her forehead with it, her large eyes staring in rapt fascination at the cards. Calvin watches her with some concern. Eventually he calls out, "Mary!" very sharply as if in an effort to break her trancelike state.

Mary tears her eyes from the cards and stares at him, smiling a little and wetting her lips. She shudders and, with obvious effort, pulls herself together.

"Excuse me," she says, and she leaves the table.

When she is gone, Calvin Jewett shakes his head. "I'm sorry," he says. "I was afraid this would happen." The opposition is rightfully suspicious and, of course, asks him what he means by that. Calvin explains that it's the way she reacts to important games. "It's completely compulsive, according to her psychiatrist, and nothing can be done about it." Then he adds, somewhat miserably but trying to bear up, "It's as if the game were—well—a sensual thing."

The Jewetts' opposition usually think it is a ploy of some sort, but they are not prepared for the Mary who returns, because she has taken off the shielding undergarments and has unloosened her hair, which now falls about her shoulders. She also has added drops to her eyes which make them bright and feverish-looking, and she has livened up her lip rouge. As she bids, her voice turns sultry and seductive, her glances to the male enemy are almost leering, and as the game progresses, her knee or foot more than once "accidentally" brushes the opposing man or men.

Even though Mary always wears a flesh-colored body stocking, the see-through blouse gives the impression that there is nothing but bare skin beneath, and this wrecks the game for the opposition. If East and West are both males, they are bound to be affected—even if only to sympathize with Calvin or to react with anger at their own reactions, which take their minds off the game, even though they may believe it is a trick.

The point is, Mary's beauty cannot be denied, her actions cannot be ignored, and if one of the opposition is the wife, then the wife is angry with Mary and will, before it is over, be furious with her helpless husband who has, through no fault of his own, become disconcerted by this ravishing creature at his side.

The upshot of all this is that the Jewetts, who are now calling the plays, end up having things pretty much their way, Mary recovering from her "wantonness" once the game is won. The opponents have no redress; there are no rules governing attire. It is a matter of tit for tat, so to speak.

Mary has taken off the shielding undergarments and has unloosened her hair. Her eyes have become bright and feverish-looking, and she has livened up her rouge. The opponents have no redress. It is a matter of tit for tat, so to speak.

Underhanded Bridge

NONSENSE TIME

Jewett and Dunstable don't always win, even with the mischief they create, but they are successful more times than not. Some of their highly abstruse exchanges have been more successful in putting their opponents off-stride than have their carefully-plotted routines, which are calculated to arouse only dander. Here is an example of an obfuscatory exchange that nettles East/West:

NORTH: I don't think an overbidder should be allowed to think he is playing with an underbidder, do you?

SOUTH: No, but a player *has* to be an underbidder in order to make it with an overbidder.

NORTH: Yes, but if the overbidder thinks he's matched with an underbidder, won't he become an even worse overbidder?

SOUTH: Not if the underbidder becomes aware of it and overbids.

NORTH: Then the underbidder will become an even worse overbidder than the overbidder if he thinks the real overbidder isn't overbidding enough.

SOUTH: Unless the overbidder underbids.

NORTH: But wouldn't that make him the underbidder?

SOUTH: Of course, in which case the former underbidder would have to overbid in order to even things out with the underbidder, though it would be best if he didn't know as the now overbidder he is playing with is an underbidder, as you've said.

Here is another:

NORTH: I never cease to be amazed by the inferences that can be drawn even from little things in bridge, provided the average player is alert and knows what to look for.

SOUTH: For example, partner.

NORTH: Well, think of the information to be gained from a person's playing a neutral card.

SOUTH: Yes, that would be highly inferential, to be sure. Only one deduction can be made from that.

NORTH: And that is. . . ?

SOUTH: That he evidently had this particular card.

NORTH: Exactly. On the other hand, one could also have made a deduction based on evidence in the event that he could not have played such a card.

SOUTH: And that is. . . ?

NORTH: That he has a void in that suit.

SOUTH: Yes. Either way the alert player examines, weighs, and acts on such information, inferring and deducing his way to game, though in each case the information would be different. Inferences are amazing, all right.

One final exchange:

NORTH: They talk about odds when they should talk about people.

SOUTH: Who, partner?

NORTH: The experts. It's people who make bridge and it's people, not mathematical probabilities, that make the true odds.

SOUTH: Faces alter cases, I always say.

NORTH: Exactly.

SOUTH: When in doubt, double the man.

NORTH: Yes, *never* double the contract.

SOUTH: Be a good people analyzer.

NORTH: [*Significantly*] Exactly.

Following this exchange, East/West never know, as they're being doubled, whether it's because they're in a bad contract or if it's because their opponents have weighed them and found them wanting.

Underhanded Bridge

ODD LOTS AND SORTS

I have heard players at my table say some of the strangest things. What they said used to bother me, but now I realize the value of the remarks lay in my reaction to them, which was usually studied preoccupation, so now I concentrate on my cards and the game and close my ears to what the enemy is trying to do to my mind.

Some of the things I've heard that have gotten to me are these:

—"No man has a perfect mind. There's always a margin for error. Don't you agree?" So I wait for the partner to answer, trying to figure it out myself, little realizing that, in the process, I've fallen into their trap.

—"Dorothy Hayden says the average player makes about a hundred mistakes in bidding and playing in an afternoon of bridge. Is that true, do you think?" I'm off and running. How many mistakes have I already made in this session? The biggest one (and the enemy's snickers and crooked smiles bear this out) is listening to these mind-twisters and getting hung up on their questions to each other.

Once, when my partner and I were playing slowly because it was a six hearts doubled and the going was rough, the opposition ruined the game when East said to West, "Did you know that at an international tournament Pierre Ghestem and René Bacherich of France once took forty minutes to bid and play one deal, including fifteen minutes for the play of one card?"

If my partner and I had objected to this observation, our opposition could have objected to our slow play, so there was nothing to do but take it and let it rankle us, which it did. We lost.

How to Set Up Roadblocks and Detours

Sometimes the snide things people do to get you off-balance at tournaments, and to a lesser extent at rubber bridge, you can do nothing about. I have seen partners invent tics of various sorts, to say nothing of twitches and scratches that prove to be disconcerting because you soon find yourself beginning to itch and scratch. There are times when I have felt that the tics were really ways of illegally communicating; at other times I have been sure they were because the tics miraculously vanished after game time, though claims can be made that the tics are caused by the tension of play.

I have seen players wear clothes that didn't match, the uncomplementary colors fairly screaming at me and interfering with my concentration. The worst case of this I ever saw was a Dayglo tie; it was the most god-awful brilliant pink I have ever seen and it bothered everybody at the table, including the Dayglo tie's partner, who was faced with it straight on throughout the entire match.

7
Diversions

Powell's Second Life

Guy Powell is a natty dresser, wears a neatly-trimmed mustache and an air of elegance. He looks as if he's always had it easy, for there's a softness about him. You'd swear he was born rich, vacationed on the Riviera, and frequently took to the baths at Baden-Baden and the cure at La Costa.

When asked what he does, Guy Powell usually says he's a curator of a museum. In a way, he's right. He's the effigy maintenance man for a Southern California wax museum—one of those places that exhibit startlingly lifelike figures of movie stars and hatchet murderers.

He is also currently president of the American Effigialogical Society. There is very little about wax Guy Powell doesn't know. He has several patents and he knows the secret of how to make wax statues look so real they seem to be breathing.

They're not breathing. But for years Guy Powell had wished they were, for he was one of the loneliest men in the world (having to consort with these mute figures all the time) until he found the world of rubber bridge.

In the museum now he has an added occupation. He schemes about how he's going to win games. And win he does. How? By being a master of diversion—and diversion can be most helpful (sometimes even necessary) if one wants to wind up on the winning side, and winning is important to Powell.

Powell's opponents never realize after playing him that they have been "Powellized." It keeps Powell happy and sane among all those scary wax figures, so don't judge him too harshly. He's not a bad person, really. He's just not lonely anymore, and he wants to keep it that way.

In case you didn't know, a diversion, in the military sense, is an attack or feint intended to divert the enemy from the point where the full-scale attack is to be made. Powell doesn't use diversion quite this way. With Powell it is more of a deflecting or delaying device that gives him or his partner (or both) a temporary advantage. And that is all that any bridge player needs.

Operating alone if he has to, but preferring a cooperative partner, Powell's technique is simply to get his opponents flustered while he and his partner relax and plan their next moves or try to regain their strength. It can be done by getting the enemy involved in a crucial question or in a pursuit to determine a propriety, legality, or procedure of one kind or another. And it is the perfect counterweight for those wordlessly dull, quiet hours in the wax museum.

For example, during the cut, if Powell's right-hand opponent fails to place the cut portion of the pack on the table on *his*

(Powell's) side of the remainder of the pack as he should (or even if he *does* do it), Powell may, before he picks up the cards to deal, claim that the cut wasn't made correctly.

A discussion is the inevitable result, and Law 5:The Cut is discussed and (if Powell has his way) read. Powell apologizes. It's not that he doesn't trust his RHO, but there are rules and he believes "Rules were made to be followed."

"But I cut the cards right," his RHO will probably say. "I know I did. I always do. And I put them on your side of the pack." There is, of course, no way to prove it.

Again Powell apologizes. "I'm sorry, but you only *think* you did. I was watching." And of course there is a new shuffle (by the same shuffler, Powell's LHO) and a new cut (by Powell's RHO, who watches his p's and q's this time).

Since Powell knew what he was going to do, the only ones with anger or frayed nerves are the opponents, which helps Powell's calm, steady game.

Sometimes, just to rankle the opposition, if Powell's partner is in on it, he will, before Powell picks up the pack, demand a new shuffle, and there is a discussion of Rule 6: New Cut—New Shuffle, the result being a reshuffle (because any player can demand one if he wants it). Also, to vary things, Powell's partner may also demand a new shuffle *after* Powell has picked up the cards, in which case Powell, the dealer, shuffles the cards per Rule 6.

If Powell and his partner find themselves losing, they usually change the pace and the run of points by mentioning an irregularity—real or imagined—and this "irregularity" must be dealt with summarily by referring to Law 13: Procedure Following an Irregularity.

The infringement, or whatever Powell says it is, halts the

game completely, stirs up the opposition, and gives Powell and his partner a chance to collect themselves. If they are losing heavily, they can use the breather.

Powell's success can be attributed to the fact that most bridge players aren't all that familiar with the fine points of play. The average player is conscientious, but he is also set in his game habits. When an unpredictable action is introduced, such as Powell's claims of "irregularities," this kind of player is dismayed and usually becomes so unsure of himself that his game is weakened.

ANOTHER POWELL ARTIFICE

Before the auction closes, Law 20 states, a player is entitled to have all previous calls restated when it is his turn to call. You guessed it: Powell never seems to hear the bids in their right order, and one of the opponents is forever having to tell him what they were. If Powell's partner is cooperating, he may complicate things by correcting "errors" in restatement which aren't errors at all but which throw the process into confusion.

Powell then informs the following bidder (RHO) that if he wishes he may, according to Rule 21, change his bid, which only compounds the chaos, all of which Powell created. Assuming Powell is South, it could go something like this:

WEST: One spade.
NORTH: Two diamonds.
EAST: Two spades.
SOUTH: Pass.
WEST: Three spades.
NORTH: Double.

EAST: Four spades.

It is obvious East/West have the advantage in cards and are on their way to slam. To avert this and to throw East/West off balance, South then calls for a review of the bidding, whereupon East or West must comply with the request.

Even if East or West reviews the bidding correctly, North can say he bid two hearts, not two diamonds, saying, "You must have heard wrong," whereupon South says to East, "You may change your call if you wish. It's in the rules." And Powell reaches for his rulebook.

"But I don't want to change my bid!" East will protest.

"Oh," South (Powell) says. "Well, in that case it seems you people have it for four spades." He looks to North. "It'll be your lead." Then to West: "You bid the spades first, didn't you?"

Most bridge players will let this larceny go at that, East laying down the dummy without realizing that they have all ignored the final three required passes, unless East has unusual strength, whereupon he may demand that the required calls be made. In this case West will probably think East is merely trying to do Powell one better by sticking to the book and, when South quickly passes, may pass himself, thinking that since North doubled three spades, when North doubles again it will leave it up to East to go to slam or redouble if he so desires.

Of course North passes, leaving East/West to make only four spades undoubled (120) with perhaps two overtricks (60), assuming they are vulnerable, which is a hell of a lot better than the 750 or 1,500 points East/West might have made in addition to their rubber points.

It is North's double that made the play possible for South. The double, which meant nothing, since East and West were going to game anyway, will puzzle East/West, as will North's denial of having bid diamonds.

What does North have? Diamonds? It is entirely possible that East/West are so thoroughly confused by this time that they might not even make the four spades, especially if West isn't sure now where the hearts and diamonds are for finesses, if and when they are needed.

THE PHANTOM DOUBLER

Sometimes wax expert Guy Powell uses Rule 41 to confuse the opposition, working it alone or with his partner.

If during the bidding Powell or his partner (North) has doubled, he will wait until the end of the auction to ask for a review of the bidding before play. If the opponents begin to do so, Powell's partner points out that it is too late, the auction is closed, all Powell can be told is what the contract is and whether or not it was doubled, and one of the opponents then proceeds to do this.

"You mean four spades [or whatever] was doubled?" Powell will ask in amazement, although he had himself done the doubling (or North had) only a short time before. He will continue, grumbling, "I sure would like to know by whom."

Where does East/West stand? They, you may be sure, are unsure.

In the event that either East or West has doubled, the same procedure is followed, with Powell registering his surprise at the double, which indicates more power than he has in his hand and helps his game by unsettling East/West.

As another tactic Powell uses colloquialisms to his advantage, forcing opponents to ask their meaning, which leaves Powell center stage to interpret and convey strength or pretend weakness or allude to a cleverness (and a superiority) that he alone seems to possess.

Underhanded Bridge

Powell will say, "It's always a pleasure to biff [trump the suit led]," or during bidding, "I'll kick it," which is usually greeted with blank stares until he explains (as if they're idiots) that he's doubling five clubs (or whatever). If he says he'll "sock it," it means the same thing.

"I don't like stiffs," he'll say, meaning he doesn't like to hold an honor without guards (it has no connection with the figures in his museum), or "such rags," meaning low cards.

He will say, "I guess I'll pump it with two spades," which means he wants to go to game (without fancy maneuvers), and if someone objects, he will protest that these little colloquialisms are accepted everywhere and expresses amazement and disappointment when East or West gets fed up with his referring to finesses as "hooks," games as "frames" ("Must be a carryover from bowling days, whoever started that!"), and "horse and horse" or "neck and neck" (meaning both sides are vulnerable).

Bridge being the polite game it is, people tolerate the Powells involved in it, assuming that they will some day mature beyond such pettifoggery (which they eventually recognize it to be). And this is all right with players like Guy Powell. They're always thinking up something new.

The last routine I saw Powell pull to divert play was to fall asleep during the bidding and to snore loudly when he was dummy. I have yet to see his point here, though I suppose the opposition becomes disconcerted when they have to wake him and tell him what night it is, what the score is, and how the last hand was played.

Once, when Powell was "wakened," he sat up and said, "I bid two beers," then grinned and asked, "Anybody want to bid two bourbons?" When no one laughed, he said, "If I pass, will anybody consider that a response?" When no reaction was forthcoming, Powell said, "It is my learned opinion that the skill of bridge is having an exact knowledge of the odds involved in the breaks of suits." He studied his hand and said, "Three no trump." And he made it, because everyone thought he was just acting silly. Some bridge groups just don't appreciate wry or off-beat humor.

If a statement must be made about the Powells of this world, it might be said that one never knows where he stands, that you never know what they (the Powells) are going to do next. That is the way it is with wax experts. They wax unpredictable.

Rock, Puccini, and Pizza

Guy Powell has by no means a monopoly on the art of diversion. Players everywhere are consciously or unconsciously misleading their adversaries.

Should rock and roll be the proper background music for two bridge players from the university's music department?

Should you lower or raise the thermostat setting to render the opposing players uncomfortable?

Should you have lights so garish they bring out every wrinkle and every hair that's out of place for players who are battling age or are worried about their physical image?

Should lamps be arranged for East/West so that they will shine in their eyes or reflect off their plastic cards?

These things happen. A little Puccini, for a Puccini lover, will absolutely destroy his game; his or her tears will probably ruin the cards, too, to say nothing of the surface of the bridge table.

Then there is always the pizza and beer that is served just before the last (and decisive) rubber and always served to the dieting guests. Either way they lose (and play badly). If they eat, they feel guilt-stricken and they hate themselves; if they don't eat, their gastric juices eat up their stomachs as they watch you lick your lips over the three delicious slices of Italian pizza you are putting away.

In fact, a discussion of ways of preparing almond duck, carbonade of beef flamande, and lobster sauté with tarragon can have a devastating effect on the dieter's game. It must be remembered here that their weight and shape is *their* problem, not yours. So no guilt feelings, please.

Then there are drinks. Alcohol helps *you* if you are the one not drinking or the one who is going easy while you are supplying your opponents with all they need. Assume they're bashful; after all, you're the host and you want them to be uninhibited in their bidding, right? Besides, if the play is for money, anything that will lower their threshold of awareness is a plus factor for you. They're adults, aren't they? They know that as well as you do. After all, you and your clear-headed partner can always drink to celebrate after the losers have gone home.

Using Their Egos

The most successful diversions are those that capitalize on the egotism of the opposition. Most people who have been through analysis will never tell you that it is money tossed down the drain. In bridge anybody who has played three games is an expert, so always assume that East and West are more experienced than you and your partner. Also assume that either one will be willing to answer your rather naive queries about the game.

In answering, these players get so puffed up that they get

topheavy and usually play miserably because they can't live up to the answers they have given you. The only real problem here is getting them to shut up once you get them going. However, the pompous are proud, and you know what that goeth before.

Here are some dandy entries into the swell-headed sweepstakes:

—"I have heard that skill means the ability of the player, that by his own knowledge and grasp of the game he can affect the final outcome. Have you found that to be true?" The secret in asking questions of this sort is making them sound profound when they are really either meaningless or obvious. Remember: *You* will not be thought a simpleton for asking the Great One *anything*, no matter how absurd.

—"Each deal of the cards is independent of how the cards were dealt the last time, so I've heard. If they've been dealt before, how can it be really as if the cards had never been dealt before?"

—"Is there such a thing as a chicken coup or was somebody kidding me?"

—"In mathematical assumptions relative to bridge cards, is it really true that a player can have n specified cards in nCn $(52n)C(13-n)$ ways?"

—"Do you believe in the efficacy of the obligatory finesse?"

—"Is it true that penalties stand, even though at some later date they have been adjudged incorrect?"

—"Do you believe the skill of bridge is having an exact knowledge of the odds involved in breaks of suits?"

—"Would you say, theoretically, anyway, that the better player should beat the less skillful, assuming all other things are equal?"

—"What do you think of the leghorn diamond?"

—"I've heard that monkeys could play bridge if they had

electrodes implanted in the right places in their brains and were tied to a computer. Is this true?"

Use these and you're off to a good game. Your prideful opponents can hardly think badly of you if you win. After all, didn't you solicit their advice? It was their answers to your questions that helped your game. Why should you deny it if they say it? If you lose, you can blame them for the same reason.

8

How Systems Can Work for You

Clyde Waite is an amateur cheater and will always remain one because he thinks he is fooling everybody. He's a big guy with whom you wouldn't want to argue, he has a midwestern twang, and pronounces all his *r*'s hard. You can always tell when he's got a good hand because he sings it out, "One *spade!*" and immediately takes the stance of one who can go through to game if not a small slam ("Partner, there's more where that came from").

If he is less jubilant or hesitates and then passes, everybody knows he's got maybe ten to thirteen points with equal distribution and doesn't want to be a game hog ("I'd rather you do the bidding this time, partner").

If he has six to nine points, he's likely to say, "Who dealt this mess?" When he doubles in a voice he'd use if he found your hand in his cash register, you don't need a flare to light the scene ("We got 'em, partner; they'll never make it").

Underhanded Bridge

Clyde's actions are unsophisticated, transparent, and unethical (even if they are, in a paradoxical way, honest). An experienced opponent never objects to Clyde Waite's manner of bidding, particularly in a money game, because he learns as much from it as does Clyde's partner.

Almost every bridge book exhorts the reader to refrain from attaching any significance to another player's actions or take such "unfair" advantage of him as to notice little idiosyncrasies or personal peculiarities that will tell you what kind of player he is and give some hint of what kind of cards he might be holding.

This is hogwash. By all means, get to know your fellow players—preferably before you meet them—and most important: *before they get to know you.* Compile a dossier, if you think that will help. The FBI does.

The "help" books emphasize the proprieties and view with horror the idea that anyone would ever watch anyone else arrange his cards or attach any significance to the way he tightens up when he has a good hand as opposed to the way he acts when he has a bad one. Again, hogwash. Look at your opponent and observe everything he does *because you can be damn sure he's been studying you.*

One ought to develop the habit of observing how the other person deals, where he places his cards in his hand, how he reacts to good cards and to bad. Believe me, it is the trustful players—and those who take the rules seriously—who get it in the neck. Remember, it's a hard, cruel world out there, and the bridge arena, for all its phony protestations of existing far from the jungle, is just as savage an adjunct.

Bridge books notwithstanding, if you play a card next to the one at the end of your hand, you can bet everybody else at the table notices it and surmises that you have one more of that suit left. You can make book on it if the game stakes are high.

In duplicate the players become so highly sensitive to what others are doing that the slightest irregularity results in the call for the director to straighten them out. Follow their example. The unaware player is a sure loser.

Do you suppose nobody objected to the first overcall or takeout double? They were forms of cheating that the perpetrators tried to get away with, but now this "cheating" has become acceptable and conventional because both sides know what they mean.

The systems of play become complex, indeed, when one considers the Rubin Transfer, the South African Texas, the Splinter Bid and the Flannery Two Diamonds.* Who can keep track of all the newer, more exotic systems of partner communication without spending his full time at it? The opponents may say that they play the Lea System.** Will you ask what it is, thereby letting them know that you don't know? If you do ask, will you understand it, even if they explain it?

---

* The Rubin Transfer is a bidding system created by Ira Rubin which prevents the opposition from utilizing an easy sacrifice against slam or game; South African Texas is an enabling transfer maneuver for level-four bids created by David Carter and developed independently in South Africa; the Splinter Bid is an antifragment or singleton-showing bid often confused with the fragment; the Flannery Two Diamonds is a bidding system developed by William Flannery to show an 11 to 15-point hand containing 5 hearts and 4 spades.

** The Lea System is a one-club maneuver invented by Robert H. Lea of Denver, Colorado, wherein one club is bid with hands of 12 or more points.

Underhanded Bridge

Simple Systems Win Out

A far simpler way to play the game is to ignore the fancy conventions and use systems that you find will work for you. For example, keep your eyes on the shuffler to see what you can see (among other things, is he really shuffling?); you may be rewarded when the careless dealer lets you see who is getting what. It beats the Schenken System* all to hell. At the very least you may get to know what the bottom card is, which will be the dealer's. It could be the card that will save your contract.

If you get in a game with poor players, try not to lower yourself to their level, but play your best. It is wiser to seek out opponents who are better than you are so that your own level of play will be raised.

The ordinary bridge fiend is satisfied to clash with others at his individual (or his partner's) level of excellence without resorting to deceits (except those encountered and sanctioned for normal play, such as false carding), especially when the play is for the simple thrill of competition or only for small stakes.

When the price of bridge goes up, however, humanity being what it is, deception becomes more commonplace, and the higher the stakes the more probable and bizarre the trickery. I have seen players hold cards in their left hands when they have good minor suits, in their right hands when they have strong major suits. I have heard people resort to strange ways of talking as they arrange their cards, mentioning to their partner, "Oh, I forgot to tell you about Uncle Elbert's angina. He's in the

---

* The Schenken System is a complicated artificial one-club bidding device devised by Howard Schenken of New York City which may or may not use both the Stayman and the nonforcing Stayman conventions.

hospital with it again," meaning, "I've got the hearts, have you got the support?" Or, "He's on a field trip again, this time to Arizona, looking for shale for oil," meaning, "I'm looking for diamonds." Or "I've been invited, but I don't think I'll join Valencia; the initiation fees are too high," meaning, "I have a void in clubs." Many players tune out such small talk to concentrate on the game, but the game may be in the small talk if you can decipher it.

The Edgeley System

Matt Edgeley has a fine system of communication worked out, and it has won him and his partner many games and much money. Somebody said if you want to hide something, leave it in plain sight. That is the way it is with Edgeley. He is a whistler and a hummer. He hardly ever talks except to bid. The rest of the time he's whistling between his teeth or humming softly.

It is quite annoying, but most opponents, after getting over their initial irritation with Edgeley (and listening to make sure he isn't communicating in any way), go along with him and ignore his bad habit. After all, that is Matt Edgeley, isn't it? How could he possibly communicate anything with "San Antonio Rose," "Old Man River," and "Kansas City Kitty?"

But Edgeley *is* communicating. "Chinese Lullaby" and other innocuous tunes are hummed or whistled when he has no message, but when he wants to impart some vital information, he segues into "I Won't Dance" (I don't want to bid), "Autumn in New York" (I've got less than ten points), "When the Red Red Robin Comes Bob-Bob Bobbin' Along" (I've got the hearts if you've got the fit), "Coax Me a Little Bit" (If you've got anything at all, bid it), "Into Each Life Some Rain Must Fall" (I've just been dealt a lousy hand), and "Skater's Waltz" (Partner, we're on thin ice with that bid of yours).

The variations are, of course, endless. When Edgeley has a pianola or a practical lay-down, he'll hum "I've Got Those Piano Roll Blues." For a hand slightly less good, "I've Got a Lovely Bunch of Coconuts." For a complete bust he'll hum "I've Got a Right to Sing the Blues."

Sometimes, when he's questioned about what he is humming, Edgeley is affronted and immediately starts humming tunes only his partner will understand, for Edgeley's repertoire is inexhaustible. For a low-count hand, Edgeley will hum the brief aria *"Ma se me'è forza perdeti"* ("But for me life is finished") from Verdi's *A Masked Ball.* Or he'll whistle the soprano aria *"Je dis que rien ne m'epouvante"* ("I said naught should frighten me here") from *Carmen* if he has a good hand. If he has a monster hand, Edgeley can be heard whistling the tenor aria from *Il Trovatore*, *"Mal regendo all 'aspro assalto"* ("At my mercy lay the foe"), and he and his partner will go to slam.

Edgely says taken pigeons are practically dead ones. Charming cheats like Edgeley have nothing but scorn for easy marks. So *"Habet Acht"* ("Beware")—that's an aria from *Tristan and Isolde.* Better take it to heart.

The Harrison Systems

I know a couple named Harrison who adopt a different system of *not* bidding for each bridge session, deciding what it will be in advance of play. This system of passing is not violating any rule since the Harrisons are communicating nothing to one another.

Sometimes they pass every other hand regardless of what they hold, playing the intervening hands normally. This proves enormously disconcerting to the opposition, and their bidding goes to hell (they overbid in the face of no opposition and underbid when the Harrisons play normally).

The opposition usually figures out what is going on by the time they meet with the Harrisons again, and then they're ready for them, but the Harrisons keep track, and on their second meeting with the same players they pass the first, fourth, seventh, and tenth hands, etc., which leaves the opposition stumbling once again.

At the next get-together they may pass only every other time on even (or odd) hours, not pass at all (the entire session), bid only odd numbers (one spade, three hearts, etc.), or even numbers (two spades, four hearts), depending upon their hands. Such systems have their dangers, but the Harrisons claim it puts their antagonists off because to them there is no recognizable system.

If their opponents demand to know what the Harrisons are doing, the Harrisons usually tell them they have abandoned all normal conventions and are merely bidding suit strengths with proper responses. Sometimes they say they are trying out ESP. The ESP explanation is the more accepted; it also renders the Harrisons more formidable as opponents since an unknown quantity has been introduced into the equation, and this factor looms larger than it should in their opponents' imaginations.

Sometimes the Harrisons will bid one over the opening bid of their opponents (if it is not too high) regardless of their count, their strength in that suit, or the quality of their hands. This robs the enemy of an intelligent, decipherable response. It is usually interpreted as a simple overcall, or even a lead-inhibiting bid, which is all to the good because their opponents will be frantically trying to find a fit and bidding far higher than they should, while the Harrisons, abandoning the move immediately after it is made, will bid normally from then on.

Sometimes the Harrisons say they are trying out ESP. This explanation renders them more formidable as opponents, since an unknown quantity has been introduced into the equation, and this factor looms larger than it should in their opponents' imaginations.

When questioned, the Harrisons say they call this the Harrison Phantom Overcall, and they have found this quite acceptable in bridge circles. In duplicate they even list it on their convention card and have been known to alert with it. But alerting here has no meaning because the overcall is mechanical and the opposition has no way of knowing how the bidder is fixed in the opening bid suit except as the bidding proceeds.

9
Making Adroit Maneuvers

Use Rules to Your Advantage

Let us assume that you are put in a game with a partner you don't like simply because the partnerships have been verbally agreed upon informally, though you have not objected up to this point because you didn't want to seem to be a cad. You can always get out of it by pointing out that Law 3 directs how partnerships are formed (the two drawing the highest cards) and that this way is the only fair way to go. While it is true you may end up with the same person (one chance in three), no one can fault you for sticking to the rules, and no one's feelings will be hurt.

If you end up with the same partner and he proves to be a liability because he doesn't seem to know what he's doing and you come up with a hand that could make a killing, *bid out of rotation at the first opportunity.* This will silence him because

Law 31, Bid Out of Rotation, takes him out of the bidding entirely; he must pass all bids because of your "mistake."

Let us assume you (South) are the declarer and, though there are other cards not yet played, the cards of the trump suit left in your hand and dummy's lie as follows:

NORTH
A Q

WEST   EAST
K and/or 10   K and/or 10

SOUTH
4

The lead is from dummy, and you need to make both the ace and queen good in order to make your contract, which has been doubled and redoubled and you're vulnerable. You have carefully kept track of the cards and know that in this suit only the trump king and ten remain out. Assuming equal distribution, East and West have one trump each. But which one has the all-important king? What do you do to find out?

You study your hand and the dummy's for a long time, then you *start to lead from your hand.*

West objects. "You're in dummy," he says quickly, and probably with some urgency. At once you know he has the king and you know the odds are that he would not also have the ten. If West did not have the king, neither East nor West would have said anything so quickly or with such urgency. As a result, you correctly surmise that the cards as situated thus:

                        NORTH
                         A Q
WEST   EAST
 K   SOUTH   10
                          4

"Oh, thank you," you say, leading the ace from dummy and taking his king, making your queen good at any time during the rest of the game and also retaining the lead, if that's important to you at this juncture.

If you have a singleton in any suit, there is nothing wrong in hesitating for a moment, as if trying to decide which among the "two or more cards" you have you will choose to play.

When you have a strong hand, you can prove how ethical a player you are (and still win) by taking yourself out of the bidding because your partner has hesitated (whether he has or not), which indicates to him that he can bid as high as he wishes in his no trump suit (or whatever, if you have the fit for his hand).

If things are going badly for you and your partner and it would be of advantage to call out of rotation, by all means do so. The least that can happen is that an opponent calls attention to it and thereby cancels it (Law 29). In the event that your LHO continues the bidding, he in effect condones and legalizes your bid, which is what you hope will happen.

Sometimes leading out of turn can work to your advantage. In many cases your lead will be treated as a correct lead if the declarer or either defender accepts it or plays a card before attention is drawn to the irregularity, thus condoning and legalizing the play.

BE A STRIPED-TAIL APE

Don't be afraid to be a striped-tail ape by making a lead-inhibiting double when the opposition is headed for a slam contract. The double may stop them in their tracks (and their score will then be small), but don't be ashamed if they go on to bid slam and you flee (as John Lowenthal mentioned in a *Bridge Journal* article*) "like a striped-tail ape in the face of a redouble." No one can say you didn't try. You can even employ this technique at the small slam level with good results—fleeing or otherwise.

It is a good idea to place singletons anywhere except at the end of your hand. Why? Because *they* are watching. While most players have 20/20 vision, they seem unable to read the rules about ethics.

Speaking of ethics, at rubber bridge talk about the proprieties, telling everyone at the table that you are sure that all infringements of bridge laws are inadvertent, that the penalties are merely provided to indemnify nonoffenders against loss as a result of such thoughtlessness. Always speak highly of players and allude to their innocence.

Then, at a crucial point in bidding (or at an advantageous pre-bid point) draw attention to some part of your own or your

---

* The "Striped-Tail Ape Double" is listed in *The Official Encyclopedia of Bridge* (New York: Crown, 1971). It points out that the doubled contract with overtricks scores less than the score for bidding and making the slam, and credits Mr. Lowenthal of Hackensack, New Jersey and cites the *Bridge Journal* article as well.

host's house (a painting, perhaps), which will make everyone turn to look at the named object.

Your partner, of course, is clued in, so he turns around so that you can see his cards. As you have been a touter of ethics, in the interests of propriety the opposition won't look at your partner's cards, but by all means don't you do what they do. *Take a good look.*

If there is any criticism, point out that you, of course, didn't look at your partner's hand any more than they did and you are disappointed to think that they would even mention such a thing, but you won't press for a penalty. Your partner can back you up by pointing out that you have always been a supporter of the proprieties, citing your recent remarks about fair play and good sportsmanship at bridge.

In such skulduggery there is triumph.

10
Devices—Infernal and External

Beyond the Geneva Convention

There is a man named Stewart Del Valle who lives on the Palos Verdes Peninsula in Southern California and collects rare works of art. He is also an expert on the lyrical *air de cour* of late sixteenth-century France. One would, therefore, hardly expect him to be either a high roller at Harrah's at Lake Tahoe or to resort to one of the wickedest ways of gaining an advantage in bridge that has come to my attention.

When the willing two dollars-a-point (or more) contenders come to Stewart's palatial home for the afternoon or evening, they know it's going to be rough, for Stewart's reputation gets around, but the challengers have no idea of how really bad it's going to get before it's all over.

Underhanded Bridge

Stewart is a recognized eccentric, so when he offers them baked beans before play, extolling the protein-rich virtue of the bean as opposed to meat and milk, and he thrusts a dessert of prunes and bananas with whipped cream upon them, the new players shrug it off as they eat. When play is commenced, they find raisins and nuts handy at the table.

When Stewart and his partner go on about vitamins and the value of good health, partaking heartily of everything, the strangers go along with it and eat their fill. Maybe all this health food will help their play and keep them alert, they think.

What they eat, however, is a deadly combination, for an hour later the two visiting firemen are shifting uncomfortably in their chairs; the formation of internal gas is perfectly normal as a result of consuming those ingredients, but intestinal gripes and flatulence in company (and in such a splendid setting!) is embarrassing. What it does mostly, however, is play havoc with one's concentration.

The beaming Stewart Del Valle and his partner find it easy to wrest the advantage from their squirming contenders. And though Stewart and partner are the perpetrators of this purposeful production of natural gas, they are not themselves affected, for they have consumed a considerable number of capsules of activated charcoal beforehand, and this absorbs the offending flatus in the intestines and they feel no spasms or discomfort.

I would call Stewart Del Valle's mischievous menu a device to win games, and a rather devilish one it is. There are many devices that can help, some of them psychological, some that call for special equipment, though none others that I know of are as far out as Stewart Del Valle's. All have their uses.

For example, there's a player I know who, when he gets into a tight spot and needs more time to think about his game, leans against the bridge table so that his telephone pager *beeps*. This *beep* would ordinarily signal him to call in to his answering service, since his pager doesn't beep unless it's important.

Accordingly, when he takes his leave to pretend to call in, no one suspects he's working out the game problem in his head instead. The *beep* device also serves another purpose: It breaks the tempo (when he feels it is necessary) and, as every card player knows, sometimes an interruption can change the flow of the game and affect the luck of the players.

THE DEAF-MUTE SHTICK

Harold Alder and Alan Duffau make their livings playing rubber bridge on trains between Los Angeles and Las Vegas. Alder is said to be a deaf-mute, but as Alan Duffau remarks to the players they meet, the blind play bridge, so why not the deaf-and-dumb?

Why not, indeed? Players are inclined to think at first that being a deaf-mute would be a distinct disadvantage at bridge. You can't hear the timbre in a bidder's voice or the exact inflection that is so clue-heavy, for one thing; for another, you can't fool your opponents with your voicing (pretending to have more than you have, for example) or inform your partner of anything by the way you bid or double.

Not so with Alder and Duffau. They get along just great and win most of the time from those who are bound for glitter gulch with plenty of cash and are willing to try their luck at enlarging their nut before hitting the gaming tables and slots. Alder and Duffau also fleece the returnees who have either won a pile or want to try to recoup what they dropped in the casinos.

Underhanded Bridge

The reason Alder and Duffau are so victorious most of the time is that *Alder isn't a deaf-mute*. It's a device. It's their *shtick*, their routine. They figure this way: The people with whom they play are able to speak, so it is assumed that they know nothing of the deaf-and-dumb language. This leaves the trickery up to Alder and Duffau.

What happens is that during the bidding Alder uses sophisticated prearranged hand signals that look like the sign language of the deaf (and are similar), signaling, "I have twenty-three points, three aces, six spades, and a void in hearts," whereupon Duffau says, "He bids a spade."

When it is Duffau's turn, Duffau will say (for example), "Three spades," but actually signals, "I've only got six points, but I do have three spades, and one of them is the king."

And so the bidding goes, Duffau knowing exactly what Alder has in all the suits by the time the auction is over, each offering new information each time it is his turn to "bid."

Even if they become defenders because of lack of points and bidding potential, they probably could defeat the contract, but they realize they can't win all the time. So they rake in the tricks when the time and the cards are right, which is when their opponents feel optimistic and have bid high. Alder and Duffau do well with doubles and redoubles.

LANGUAGE NO BARRIER

Bert and Nancy Mica are expert bridge players who teach Russian, German, and French at two different high schools, Bert being head of the language department at his school. During the summer they move about the country drumming up rubber bridge for good stakes (and thereby paying for their vacations).

Like Alder and Duffau, they have a routine in which Nancy is said to be Bert's bride from Russia. She has yet to learn English, he says. But she has learned how to play bridge. Here's how it goes:

NANCY (North): *U menia dvatsat-odin oczkov i pjat czervey i czetyre pikovyh kart* ("I have twenty-one points and five hearts and four spades").

BERT (South): She bids a heart.

EAST: Pass.

BERT: Two hearts. [*Then to Nancy*] *Vosem oczkov, czetyre pikovyh i tri czervey* ("Eight points, four spades and three hearts").

WEST: Pass.

NANCY: *Mne nedostayot tolko trefovyi tuz.* ("I am missing only the ace of clubs").

BERT: She bids two spades.

EAST: Pass.

BERT: Three spades. [*Then to Nancy*] *Ya dumayu czto my mozem zdelat szlem* ("I think we can make a slam").

NANCY: [*After West passes*] *Govorja o bubnah; U menia tri* ("Mention diamonds; I've got three").

BERT: She says four diamonds. [Then, after East passes] Five diamonds. [*Then to Nancy*] *Prodolzaem s pikami* ("Let's stay with spades").

NANCY: [*After West passes*] *U menia pikovy korol i czervy* ("I've got the king of spades and hearts").

BERT: She says six spades.

East, South, and West pass and Nancy has it for six spades in this great language swindle.

Part of the reason this fraud is so successful is that Nancy is so cute and innocent. Here she is in a country that still must seem so very strange to her, and she is getting along so well. The opposition never guesses that she understands and can speak six languages, including English, fluently. They buy Bert's story that it took him two years to get the Soviets to let her come to America with him as his wife and then only because he'd been teaching English to the Russian cosmonauts who were chosen to work with the United States in the big bilateral space venture.

Their challengers never seem to mind losing money to the "in-love" Bert and Nancy Mica, and they all agree that Bert has done a fine job teaching Nancy bridge.

"It's not played in Russia," Bert explains. "They frown on the idea of cards with pictures of kings and queens on them."

(Actually, organized contract bridge was banned in the Soviet Union in early 1973 by the state sports committee because it was supposed to be socially harmful, though Russians may still play the game in private.)

THE RHYTHM METHODS

Anyone who has ever developed pictures in the dark or has tried to determine how far away that lightning bolt was by counting "one thousand and one, one thousand and two," which roughly approximates the seconds, will quickly understand one of the most prevalent and undetectable devices used for cheating at rubber bridge, at duplicate, and at national and international tournaments.

What it consists of is training yourself to become a metronome with your partner. You both practice "one thousand and one, one thousand and two," until your cadence counting is so together as to be one voice. Then you shut your mouth and do it in your head, bidding at the proper times after the "begin signal." This signal can be anything, from an innocuous glance at your watch (but not to see what time it is), a barely audible clearing of the throat, a lowering of your card-holding hand to the top of the table, or one signal following another and varying from hour to hour. The signal must be definite and precise so that the mental cadence counting can be started.

The most vital information to be transmitted to you (or your partner) will be point count. So you have arranged your cards (you are South), West has bid (as dealer), your partner gazes at his or her cards, and you are keeping your hand up off the table. You casually drop your hand.

One thousand and one, one thousand and two, one thousand and three, one thousand and four, one thousand and five, one thousand and six, one thousand and seven . . .

"One diamond," your partner says.

Your partner has fourteen points (figuring two points for every "second" in this cadence). In the same way you telegraph *your* point count with *your* response, whether it is a bid or a pass.

One has to be alert to play bridge in the first place, but one must be superalert to play using the cadence swindle. Signals often change during the defending aspect of the game where first-lead defender gives the agreed-upon signal that starts the cadence for his partner to indicate what suit he wants to be led, the partner beginning to count, "One thousand and one," and dropping his hand to the table (or whatever) to indicate: "Lead a club." Dropping his hand at the count of two would be diamonds, three would be hearts, and four would be spades.

OTHER TRAPS AND TREACHERY

Maneuvering can be a device, particularly if you get your opponents into positions where you can see into their hands, either directly or in mirrors. Be alert on trains, buses, and planes; make sure your opponent sits next to the window, where his hand can be reflected to your advantage. Mirrorlike sunglasses may help you if your partner wears them so you can see his cards in them, but your friend had better play a straight and stiff-headed game or others might also profit.

Anyone who has taken a test for color blindness knows that with red or green glasses the pattern of dots in seemingly random scattering in a picture suddenly stands out to form a number or a letter. Some hard-pressed players resort to wearing tinted glasses and marking card packs with a substance visible only to them so long as they're wearing the spectacles. Looking around the table, they can tell what cards everyone is holding. It is hardly sporting; indeed, it never ceases to amaze me what people will do to make a crooked nickel.

Such devices as the trick glasses and special playing cards that have the rank and suit of their faces hidden in the intricate pattern on their backs and can be read halfway across a small room by the person who knows how to do it, can be purchased at specialty houses, gambling houses, novelty shops, and magic stores. There are many varieties of trick decks, but experienced bridge players are not easily fooled by them. Truly clever perpetrators of sharp practices don't buy ready-made tricks and cheating devices.

One man I know uses a hearing aid that is actually a receiving unit for a transmitter used by his partner, who signals in morse code fashion to let him know how many points and what manner of cards he's holding. Another man uses at various times a cast on his arm or leg—even an eye patch—that receives signals sent in code by his partner.

By far the most resourceful man I know has taken to wearing a turban that conceals electronic receiving equipment that taps his scalp. When suspicious players ask him why he wears it, he replies, "Oh, this turban? I'm getting a hair transplant." Such frankness can be nothing less than completely disarming.

11
Gaining an Edge with Anger

THE GLADY METHOD

Bertram Glady knows how to get under your skin. It isn't that he doesn't like you or that he's trying to put you down because you're so uppity; it's just that Bertie, as everybody calls him, knows the value of getting the other guy angry.

"Get 'em mad," Bertie says, "and you've practically won the game."

It doesn't always work out that way, but it does work out that way often enough to make giving it a try worthwhile when other things don't seem to be working for you. Just make sure you're able to defend yourself—physically.

In the meantime, let's see how Bertie operates.

"A regular ace-grabber," he'll say if you trump the ace he's just put down. "What else you been grabbin' lately, fella?" It's up to you to interpret that remark according to the way he says it (very insinuating). Surely there's an insult there somewhere, and he's counting on you to find it.

"*Oooh!*" he'll say in his most campy style when you put down your queen. "A queen! What do you know! What closet did you spring from, honey?"

It's up to you to determine whether he's speaking to the card or to you. In other words, you can be insulted or not. Most people, especially players who don't know Bertie, take offense. And blow their game. And when they do, Bertie has some snide remark to make about that. As a result, the next game—if there is one—will be played with elevated blood pressures: the other side's, not Bertie's.

To a bigot Bertie's apt to say, "You played a spade king. How could you hold a black card like that in your lily white hand?"

The only way to handle Bertie is to laugh him off. But I've seen people get up out of their chairs, wild looks in their eyes, ready to let Bertie have it in the chops. They've always been restrained.

Bertie doesn't let it stop there, though. In his best Don Rickles manner he'll add, "Oh, getting to you, eh? Can't take it, is that it? Thought you bigots had more guts than that."

By this time the bigot target of Bertie's well-aimed arrows is fit to be tied and has to forfeit the game or play it while he seethes and suffers more barbs from Bertie's sharpened tongue.

Under those circumstances Bertie's opponents usually lose. Fortunately, Bertie is over six feet and weighs two hundred and twenty pounds (but inside he's really all jelly). I have seen contenders look him over after his insults, but nobody has ever taken him on afterward. So far.

TALKING UP TENSION

Sam Glendean is a constant talker—for a reason. He will say such a thing as, "Ever consider spades as a symbol for grave-digging, hearts for life, diamonds for wealth, and clubs for violence?" Then, without waiting for an answer, he will go on with some other bit of dull bridge arcana: "In Italy, Spain, and the Latin countries the suits are cups, coins, swords, and cudgels. Not much difference, is there? Cups hold the ashes, coins represent wealth, swords and cudgels the violence. No hearts, those people."

Then, while everybody is squirming as a result of Sam's little soliloquies, he still pushes on: "In Germany, Austria, Bohemia, Poland, and Hungary the suits are hearts, leaves, bells, and acorns. A real difference there, isn't there?"

"Knock it off, will you, Sam?" someone usually says, trying to concentrate on what they've just been dealt by Sam.

"Oh, sure. I get the message." Crestfallen, Sam will be quiet for a moment. Then: "I just want to add that in Switzerland blossoms and shields take the place of the bells and acorns."

"Sam. . . !" Exasperation.

"All right! All right!" Silence. Then: "You know, looking at these cards and remembering how it was when I was a kid, we'd be playing Old Maid or Go Fish. Young innocents we were and those were innocent games. Well, it's not like that anymore. You take Mark Goldstein of Hopkins, Minnesota, for example. He played a great game in the charity match of the Summer Nationals in 1962. And how old was he? I ask you: How old?"

"Sam, let's get with it, huh?" Pleading.

"He was seven years old, that's what he was."

Sam finally bids, but he's accomplished what he set out to do. Straining and waiting soon tires even the most patient player, and this is Sam's purpose: exhaustion.

"It's up to you, Sam. You dealt. Remember?"

"Of course I remember. And I remember something else, too. I remember that Dianne Barton of San Francisco won ten master points when she was only eleven years old. Did you know that? Imagine a kid that young——"

"Sam, for God's sake, are you ever going to get around to playing this game?"

"Oh, yeah. Sure." Hurt feelings.

Sam finally bids, but he's accomplished what he set out to do. He's gotten his opponents rattled and uncomfortable. They keep waiting for him to say, "Say, did it ever strike you as strange that in bridge . . ." and start a new line all over again. Straining and waiting like that soon tires the most patient player, and this is Sam's purpose: exhaustion.

"They're like tightened rubber bands when I get through with them," he confided to me. "I let up just before I think they might snap. You know what they're thinking about? Not the game. They're thinking about how they'd like to wring my neck." He laughed.

I asked him once why they still allowed him to get in their games if he angered them so much, making each game such a stressful thing.

"What reason would they have not to?" he replied. "I've done nothing wrong, haven't broken any rules. Bridge is a polite game. They have to be polite." He laughed again. "And I am polite. I never get mad when they bawl me out. I'm always glad when they do because then they feel guilty that they weren't polite, and you know you can't play a good game filled with guilt. Isn't that right?"

I told him he was right, and I know he is because I've seen how many points he's accrued and how much money he's taken in at rubber bridge middling stakes games.

Underhanded Bridge

Operation Inconsideration

There are other ways of making your opponents angry besides being a boor or a bore. The easiest way is to have no regard for their feelings. A lot of bridge players do that unconsciously, blowing smoke in the faces of nonsmokers, wearing perfume or cologne that's straight out of the cosmetics counter of the nearest cut-rate drugstore, smoking cheap cigars, playing with sniffly colds, constantly coughing, blowing runny noses and snatching at tissues all during play and then expecting you to deal the very cards they have been holding.

These people sometimes wonder how they managed to win those games that night. If you've ever wondered that and have done any of the above things, now you know. Your opponents were angry and didn't play well and maybe they've decided they don't like you. So it all comes down to this: Are you in it to make friends or win games? *You* must decide.

One couple I know uses a technique I haven't seen worked by anyone else. They laugh and giggle all through the game. My wife and I have played them, and everything we'd say, even to each other, caused this couple to exchange glances and giggles, and sometimes they even laughed outright.

As a couple, my wife and I aren't that funny. With a few drinks we think we are. But being perfectly sober and being laughed at is enough to rankle you, especially if you don't know *why* you are being laughed at.

It wasn't until after we'd lost to this couple repeatedly that Jean and I began to understand the routine. So now we laugh at them and they've quit laughing at us. Now *we* are winning the games. Turnabout is fair play, folks. Better think about that before you start anything funny.

Practical jokers have their place, and I'll bet you can tell me just where that is (and you are probably right). Jokers themselves can elicit rage. I know one man who slips a joker into a bridge deck whenever he can. Of course he doesn't let the players know who is responsible. It makes for antagonism—on the part of everybody but the perpetrator. It doesn't seem a fair thing to do, but once again it does win games because the others are put off by it and therefore don't play as well as they do ordinarily.

Then there is the not-so-shy pornographer who slips a deck of girlie cards or hardcore porno cards into the deal. It makes for shock, red faces, and sometimes embarrassed laughter, but it doesn't make for lasting friendships. Especially if you're the trickster. Occasionally it will win games, but it is no sure thing.

A System Backfires

One of the most insufferable boors I ever met was Homer Keeling, and of course that was his gimmick—his being arrogant and a bore and difficult to get along with. He and his partner, a subdued man named Lyle Sarles, played rubber bridge for money at a club whenever they could drum up business.

Homer was quite well-known, for he'd acquired some international match points, and his bridge was inspired. Yet he seemed to think he had to rub everybody the wrong way in order to win. Maybe that's why he did. Who can say? All I know is that he thought my partner and I should be honored to play with him. The truth was my partner and I *were* honored, but we didn't want him to know it, since he seemed to demand we tell him. We didn't like having to treat him as if he were the Holy See. Also, groveling at the feet of your opponent is not the way to begin a game.

We played Homer and Lyle and we lost. We grumbled and settled up our cent a point. "Just consider it learning money," said Homer loftily. "When you two get to where I am, you can skin the opposition,too, and tell them the same thing."

We pointed out that we'd given him a tough fight a time or two there and that we weren't beginners, and we had a few master points ourselves.

"Ha! Master points!" Homer dismissed them with almost a snarl.

"But it's those master points and what they represent that kept you from skunking us," I protested.

"Look," Homer said, "if you hadn't scored anything anywhere along the line it wouldn't have been a legitimate game. The cards break even, average ten points each hand during the evening, so the opposition always gets *something* just through luck—even beginners, and even from such masters as myself. So remember that, suckers."

That little speech proved to be Homer's undoing, for it gave me an idea. I got hold of Miles Evart (you remember Miles, the card trickster, don't you?) and asked him if he would play Homer and Lyle as my partner. I told him what I wanted him to do. He rather reluctantly agreed, but when he met Homer Keeling and found out what kind of person he was, Miles went to his work with relish.

HOMER'S LAST GAMES

We arranged to play for two cents a point, which guaranteed a crowd, and Homer was pleased with himself, thinking he'd talked us into it. He and Lyle settled down for a real match. The crowd had no idea that Miles could manipulate cards right in front of their eyes, and neither did Homer or Lyle.

The strategy Miles and I had agreed upon was to have Homer consistently dealt (and for Homer to deal himself) impossibly freakish hands—hands so good that he would become suspect in the eyes of all who were watching.

As he played, holding hand after hand with more than twenty and thirty points, Homer began to sweat. He was bidding big and making his contracts—slam after slam. We couldn't double. We couldn't bid. The crowd began to regard Homer with suspicion.

Miles and I lost two rubbers without a point while Homer and Lyle amassed a fantastic count. Then, as we had agreed, Miles did some fancy handwork as he angrily picked the deck from out of Homer's startled hands, holding the pack up to the light.

"Aha!" Miles said, looking at the card he'd taken from the top. "I see now why you win." He showed the card and distributed others to the crowd, and then he called for the club manager.

Homer's face went white. He grabbed one of the cards and held it up to the light. Little pinholes showed through, and "KS" could be seen.

"King of spades," I said. "I can see it from here."

The crowd began grumbling and making ugly remarks. The club manager came up.

"Hey now, listen——" Homer began. But the crowd wasn't listening. The manager was there, and when Miles showed him the cards and how they could be read, the manager glowered at Homer and Lyle and told them to leave.

They protested, but finally they gave up and went out, bedeviled and bewildered. They've never been back.

I felt terrible for a few moments, and even Miles seemed to think he'd gone a little far. But at the club bar feelings ran high and everybody wanted to buy our drinks. Nobody, it turned out, had ever liked Homer. They had always suspected him of some kind of shenanigans. Now it was easy to see what he'd been doing.

It didn't seem so easy to me, but I didn't say anything. Miles and I didn't dare look at each other.

What I learned from the breaking of Homer Keeling is that few people really like a winner, because a winner places himself above and apart from others. People can accept a winner who loses now and then because, like themselves, he's proved he's human. Homer didn't have sense enough to lose once in a while.

Winning and being arrogant—well, nobody likes that combination in a person. So if you're going to win, lose a little if you want to keep your friends.

12
Double Dealing

THE BUENOS AIRES AFFAIR

Two Britons, Terence Reese and Boris Schapiro, were accused of signaling to each other with their fingers at the world championship in Argentina in 1965 in what has since been referred to as The Buenos Aires Affair.

They were said to be signaling the number of hearts they held—two fingers for two or five, depending upon whether their pinkies were open or held together, three fingers for three or six, and so on.

The staid, steady bridge world was shaken by the charges, the World Bridge Federation found the two men guilty, the evidence was turned over to the British Bridge League, and it has been a cause célèbre ever since. Reports vary, but *The Official Encyclopedia of Bridge** declares that both men have been since vindicated.

* Richard Frey and Alan F. Truscott, eds., *The Official Encyclopedia of Bridge*, rev. ed. (New York: Crown, 1971).

It doesn't matter. What does matter is that the incident surfaced at all because, the mythology of the game notwithstanding, there *are* double-dealers in bridge, and not just finger signalers. Some systems are so exotic they probably never will be detected (and therefore never reported). In the main, however, working with the cards (manipulation) is probably the simplest and most prevalent method of cheating (and winning) at bridge.

What card manipulation has going for it is that you don't have to memorize anything, write out fancy scripts with which you and your partner can dazzle and befuddle your opponents, or perfect those terribly intricate split-second cadence-counting systems. All you have to do is be quick with your hands. They say the hand is quicker than the eye. If your hand is *not* quicker, you're going to be in for a lot of trouble.

Any card trick book or treatise on cheating with cards will tell you about the false overhand and the fake riffle shuffle that can work to exquisite advantage; phenomenal card palming and card substituting can be worked up to a fine art at the table as the chatter and cheating go on. I have seen cards marked right at the table, to say nothing of their being crimped, cut, and shaved.

The No-Cut Cut

One couple I know are good card mechanics, and they work the following:

South shuffles as North deals. South (the shuffler) arranges the cards the way he wants (double-deals) and puts them to his right. East, his RHO and the next dealer, offers the cards to the man at *his* right (North) when the time comes. North does a little patter as he lifts off the cards, putting them on *his* side of the pack for the cut. The dealer, East, through habit, puts them back the way the double-dealer (South) had arranged them in the first place, suspecting nothing, dealing the hands exactly as prearranged by South as a result.

It seems an awful lot of trouble to go through, but North and South, when they can get pigeons, play for a half dollar a point and up. And for good reason: They're excellent handlers, smooth and undetectable, and what's more, they can vary this routine with many other systems just as reliable and effective.

There's a man I know named Grady Funston who carries with him a little square of fine, flesh-colored sandpaper—it must be 6/0 or finer—glued to his right thumb so that when he gets into a game for high stakes, he can run the piece of sandpaper over the cards, shading the edges of the ones he's interested in as the game goes along. He works on the aces first, then the kings, queens, and jacks. When he is done, he removes the sandpaper.

When he deals, he can tell either by feel or by the fuzzy look of the edge of the cards the honor of each. At first he was satisfied merely to know whether or not a card was an ace. Now he's got it worked out so that he can rub the gritty paper in such a way that he can even tell the suit.

This seems a waste of talent when a pack of any kind of marked cards one might want are easily available at magic and novelty stores—even those you can read across a room—but most card mechanics prefer to work with the cards that are already in the game (suspicion would be aroused if they insisted upon introducing their own cards).

Underhanded Bridge

How to Read the Scene

How do you know when there's cheating going on? It's difficult, especially with good operators, but (1) when the stakes are very high, (2) when the play is with strangers, (3) when the cards don't seem to fall within normal limits in your hand (odd or freakish distribution), (4) when there are slam bids with great frequency, (5) when there are an unusual number of doubles, or (6) when *they* redouble without a qualm and go on to make it—then deception of a more sophisticated order may be working against you and your partner. Such phenomena are usually encountered at rubber and four-deal bridge (Chicago) for money you can't afford to lose.

Once I was in a game in which I saw a man dealing seconds (he was not my partner), and the game was, as a result, going badly for my partner and me. I was in a dither, not knowing what do do and not wanting to challenge, since he had already dealt and could not be caught in the act just completed. So I put one of the cards in my pocket before the play was completed and subsequently "discovered" I had too few cards. Since the card could not be found, there had to be a redeal. The double-dealer got the message. We got a new pack and honest hands for a change.

Another double-dealer I know used to bring along extra cards of the kind he knew were being used in the game and kept them "up his sleeve," so to speak, until he was losing. Then he would add the card to his hand and thereby nullify the game. He was able to keep the straightest face I have ever seen. I avoided him like the pox, and soon others did, too.

COMBATTING FRAUDULENCE

If you feel the cards you are about to deal have been fixed, you are entitled to the final shuffle (as has been mentioned earlier), which should give you a fairer shake (Law 4: The Shuffle—a pack properly prepared should not be disturbed until the dealer picks it up for his deal, at which time he is entitled to the final shuffle).

On the other hand, double-dealers who insist on the final shuffle should be watched and any irregularity pointed out at once. If you only *think* there has been an irregularity, you can demand a new cut before the first card is dealt. This nullifies any double-dealing, for the dealer's right-hand opponent must cut again (Law 6: New Cut).

A little glue sometimes comes in handy to stick two cards together to be played on an important trick. (Such waxy glue is available at magic stores.) When cards are stuck together, the final count is one card short and the trick (when the cards are found) is, by the rules, declared defective.

I have purposely damaged a card when I felt that the deck was a marked one, and I have carefully looked over the new pack that, as a result, replaced it.

Eager double-dealers sometimes distribute cards out of turn for a purpose. It must be remembered that the deal stands (according to the laws) if no one draws attention to the "error." It is always best to keep everyone on his toes and call attention to irregularities; otherwise, you may find yourself a victim— with or without knowing it.

Underhanded Bridge

BE THE SCOREKEEPER!

It is said jokingly, but there is a lot of truth to the remark that it's best to be the scorekeeper. He can add and subtract to his heart's content and no one will do anything but correct him if he is caught because all scorekeepers' mistakes are assumed to be innocent ones, bridge being the "gentleman's" game it is.

Therefore, if you are up against players who usually beat you by several hundred points at each meeting, you might try making it up by being scorekeeper, if it is that important to you. It would seem that it is the duty of all players to keep the scorekeeper honest. If they do not, it only follows that the scorekeeper will stray and become careless in favor of his side.

Remember: *L'occasion fait le larron* ("opportunity makes the thief").

13
Duplicate Duplicity

Double Trouble

There is a story that is told about a session at duplicate bridge in which the contract was played out at five hearts doubled and redoubled. When it was over, the declarer glared at his partner and grumbled, "I don't see why you had to redouble."

"Redouble?" responded the partner with astonishment. "I didn't redouble!"

"Well, I sure as hell didn't."

The winners smirked. What were their opponents trying to do, get out of their redouble penalty?

"It was Gus who redoubled," a bystander said.

"Gus?" the declarer said, turning to him.

The spectator nodded. "Sure. He always redoubles."

"Where is he?"

"He didn't like the way you were playing the hand, so he left."

The spectator shrugged. "Nobody could have made five hearts with that hand." He yawned, stretched, and then turned to go. "I was right to double."

Whether the story is true or not, it is a fact that such a thing could conceivably take place at a crowded duplicate tournament hall where cigarette and cigar smoke hangs heavy in the air and chatter and laughter and weeping all take place at the same time.

Somebody said that being a kibitzer may be the only safe form of bridge, vicarious though it is, because you can never be blamed for anything. That may be true, but if you offer gratuitous advice, bid, double, or redouble, you may find it unhealthy, though you can still kibitz with your arm in a sling or your leg in a cast.

Kibitzers can be valuable accomplices, however. Seated behind or beside a player, they can signal to partners by eye movements or nonmovements. For example, if the nonplayer looks away from the cards, the hand contains less than thirteen points; if he never takes his eyes off the cards until after the bidding is completed, the hand has more than thirteen points. It is easy to see that a number of subtle signals that convey precious information can be worked out.

The rules of duplicate contract bridge being what they are—so exacting, so complicated, the procedures so ritualized (to say nothing of all the things each player has to keep in his head, since the play and aim is different from rubber bridge)—it is a wonder the players have the time, the energy, or the inclination for deception other than that allowed under the laws.

Even those procedures are being overhauled. Because there is so much suspicion of cheating at high levels (if you lose, you tend to wonder), the diagonal bidding screen is being introduced in the final rounds of championships now. But even if such screens become *de rigueur*, it must be remembered that man is a versatile, resourceful animal and is sure to find his way around the screens. It may be time, in fact, for ESP.

On lower levels (where most of us are) there are just as many opportunities for deception in duplicate as in rubber. It is a different arena, and it has the added advantage of its aggregation of people. Intense people.

Streakers Strike Out

At a recent National Bridge Tournament in Vancouver, British Columbia, four streakers (two men and two women) ran through the game room. So intent were the players on their game that the bare flesh hardly elicited a glance from the several hundred experts who were competing in a team championship.

It is true that in duplicate one leaves the boards alone, the cards can't be fooled with, and the bidding is a stringent process, but there is also the greater possibility of distraction and intimidation, streakers notwithstanding.

For example, one man I know brings along his partner, a statuesque and well-proportioned blonde who invariably wears slit skirts or a décolleté gown that infuriates the women and rattles the men. In spite of the fact that the young woman is only an average player, the man and his partner and her eye-catching decolletages always make good points, considerably in excess of what they would earn without the scenery.

A woman player I know actually pays for hangers-on who are referred to as her entourage. She is like what she must imagine the queen mother to be: regal and condescending. Beginning players and the easily intimidated are affected by this grand show. They ask themselves, Why are those people following her every move (table to table) and her every play? Why are they all holding their breath like that? Experienced players ignore the followers and are on to her little trick, yet it is a psychological ploy that is not easily dismissed. It works its magic because of sheer numbers, the trappings, and the royal demeanor of the woman.

The rules say one should not discuss hands played (or even listen when they are discussed), but believe me, I've seen this done at all the tournaments I've attended. Sometimes the cards and bids are talked about in such loud voices at the post mortems that the East/West Team, or Pair 9, for example, can get a good idea of what's ahead of them in all the hands they have yet to play on the boards at other tables. All they have to do is keep their mouths shut and their ears open.

Getting a Wire

The term *wiring* is applied to the tournament player who leaves his table (ostensibly for a drink or to go to the bathroom) and wanders about picking up information on hands he will be playing. In other words, he gets a "wire" on the hand. He sometimes has his wife or a friend move about for him, reporting back with the valuable information gathered on the stroll.

The most unique way I've ever heard of getting a wire is to use a special hearing aid that can be turned up to pick up conversations from a remote table. This is particularly useful when one is dummy and can concentrate on the voices.

Holding up play in order to get time to think may be helpful, but if you hold up play or disrupt the so-called natural rhythm of play in fang-and-claw duplicate matches, the director is likely to be called and a penalty against you and your partner requested and possibly invoked.

A practical and permissible way to hold up play in order to catch your breath or get time to think is to use as an advantage what appears to be a disadvantage: *Call the director.* You don't have to have a reason. You merely have to state one, and any imagined irregularity will do. Who can say how fast time passes for you? It *seemed* as if your opponents were taking a long time, you say. And you can even apologize for what you labeled a "trance" or a "huddle." Nobody becomes angry with an apologizer unless he accuses without reason too many times.

A reverse ploy is slowly speeding up play so that you can ask the opposing team to kindly step up the tempo, otherwise you will be obliged to call the director.

GO FOR THE JUGULAR

It does indeed pay to know the rules so that the opposition can be pounced upon at their slightest deviation from what is acceptable. It's a jungle, remember? So hesitate not. Word will get around, however, so you must be prepared to fly right yourself.

Get the *ACBL Laws of Duplicate Contract Bridge* and study every one of them. Then, the next time you go to a tournament and you see the rules being broken left and right, you can do something about them. Your opponents can be easy prey. Go for their carotid arteries.

Mind you, this won't make friends, but as bridge pro Paul Soloway put it in a recent interview in the Los Angeles *Times*, "On the higher tournament levels a killer instinct is mandatory because so many of your competitors are friends. You can't ease up against a friend and play winning bridge."

The truth is, Soloway's philosophy applies to all levels of bridge—even to that played in the living room. Adopt it if you want to be a winner.

14
Desperation Time

A Royal Flush Saves the Day

You and your partner are in a private game over your heads. You already owe two or three hundred (thousand?) dollars you don't have and everything rides on this last rubber. You could get in deeper or, if you won, you could come out with a profit, but you have a feeling the game's been fixed and you and your partner are the pigeons. So it's desperation time. You look at your opponents and see no mercy there. In fact, you doubt they'll take your check, and you're not sure they might not take your life or break your arm, leg, or jaw when they find out you can't pay.

What to do? You look at your partner, see the hopelessness in his eyes. You both swallow nervously. You both start to perspire. You and your partner are wishing you were anywhere else. If only you had a sure-fire way of winning—or at least of getting out of there with bones and skin intact!

Calvin Jewett and Larry Dunstable, who were mentioned earlier, have more than once found themselves in such desperate straits and have worked out a routine to save life and limb that is successful for them. It goes like this:

When Jewett and Dunstable see that they're in for trouble against insurmountable odds, Jewett, at a signal, begins to develop a tremor in his hands. This would be normal in a tight game, so not much is said about it. We can assume that the opposition (East/West) think it is a sign that their victims are getting rattled, which is all to the good (not that it makes much difference, since they've got the game wired anyway).

Dunstable then begins to appear worried about Jewett and asks him, "Is there anything wrong, Calvin?"

Jewett wets his lips, swallows, shifts a little unsteadily in his chair, and shakes his head, seemingly unable to speak. He commences breathing heavily, and then somewhat raggedly and raucously.

Dunstable now says with more concern, "Cal, you don't look good."

"I don't feel good," Jewett wheezes rather dazedly, looking around. "Are there any devices around here?"

Of course the opposition wants to know what Jewett means. "Devices? What kind of devices?" They are always suspicious. East and West have no intention of letting Jewett or Dunstable off the hook with or without trickery.

"It's his pacemaker," Dunstable says, regarding Jewett with a despairing look. "Microwave ovens, radar—any kind of electromagnetic device can throw it off. He's got to be careful. Maybe there's a weather station near here or a radio relay system in operation."

By this time Jewett is trembling all over. He has to hang on to his cards with both hands. Dunstable gets up and says, "Better get you a drink of water," and proceeds to do so.

When Dunstable returns to give Jewett the glass of water, Jewett is ready. From his pocket he has taken a 100 mg tablet of niacin (nicotinic acid), which is available at any drugstore because it is completely harmless. He swallows the pill along with the water.

It takes about five minutes for the pill to operate. In the meantime, Jewett's "symptoms" become more severe. The opposition may suggest delaying the game until the shaking episode is over or may even point out that it might be more healthy if they finished the game somewhere else.

But Jewett shakes his head. "No," he says hoarsely, "we began the game, we've got to finish it."

The niacin causes flushing of the capillaries just under the skin, and the flesh turns red, often a violent, rashy red. The feeling one has is that of heated discomfort, but that is all. The flushing will, in time, go away. But the opposition doesn't know that, and, seeing Jewett's fiery red face, arms, neck, and hands, are sure that they are witness to some dread pathological process.

If the opposition does not give up the game and insist Jewett be taken to a hospital—or at least to a doctor, for he's really having a horrible shaking fit by this time—Jewett may just pretend to pass out, in which case the game must stop anyway. If the game is going in favor of Dunstable and Jewett at this juncture, however, as his color gradually returns to normal, Jewett may allow himself slowly to recover, the crucial tally going to them by virtue of a demoralized East and West.

THE CAST IS DYED

Two men I know (their names are Fridley and Givhans) have never heard of Dunstable and Jewett, yet they practice a routine similar to the aforementioned which is just as successful in extricating them from a difficult situation. All that one can assume from this is that in severe circumstances equally severe measures must be taken to end them. The only time Fridley and Givhans use this course of action is in time of extreme crisis or when they think they are being taken by dishonest players or card mechanics with muscle.

I would not endorse this method, though I have been assured by a physicians' advisory service that it is safe. I think you will admit that confronted by the phenomenon, you would comport yourself much as the opposition does in this case. When it's desperation time, here's what Fridley and Givhans do:

Fridley, who flunked out of medical school but still has connections and is now a paper salesman, excuses himself, and as he goes to the john (or whatever), the game is held up. Their opposition, of course, isn't going to let them get away with anything, so they are watchful and patient. Either Fridley returns promptly or the game will be forfeit. It isn't their fault that Fridley has chosen this time to excuse himself.

In a rest room (or anywhere handy where he is assured privacy), Fridley shoots up a little methylene blue. This is a blue aniline dye that Fridley had discovered is used in the treatment of diphtheria, malaria, and is an antidote for cyanide poisoning. It has, as far as I have been able to learn, no damaging physiological characteristics, but it does have a shocking physical result: methylene blue (injected) turns the subject a *deadly shade of green!*

When Fridley returns, therefore, they all see his green skin. Even the blood vessels in his eyes, his lips, his tongue, and gums are all green. He looks perfectly ghastly. While he feels absolutely fine, he pretends he's on his last legs.

You can imagine how shaken the opposition is by Fridley's appearance. When Fridley insists they continue to play, looking as if he'll drop dead any second, his head bobbing and weaving, his eyes fairly popping, the opponents are hardly able to finish the hand.

Of course Givhans plays along with Fridley's trickery and urges Fridley to quit, to let the opposition win because his health is more important. But Fridley won't hear of it. "Too much invested," he says harshly.

"What about your life?" Givhans asks.

"I know, I know," Fridley gasps, struggling to go on.

It is an effective act, and the opposition is always anxious to play it through (and *quickly!*) if they must play it at all. But they are also determined to get the hell out of there and away from the "dying" Fridley and Givhans lest they be accused of something. In the process they usually throw discretion to the wind, letting the ailing man and his partner take the money. Nothing is worth going through this agony, not even money.

Which only proves Machiavelli: "It has never been a wise policy to drive an enemy to desperation."

ABOUT THE AUTHOR

JERRY SOHL was born in Los Angeles, grew up in Chicago, and spent many years as an itinerant newspaperman before doing a three-and-a-half-year stint in the Army during World War II. After the war and marriage he returned to newspapering as a stringer for *Life* and *Time* and the Associated Press and also began writing novels in his spare time.

In the late 1950s he shifted to television work in Hollywood, turning out scripts for such shows as *Alfred Hitchcock Presents*, *Star Trek*, *Naked City*, *Route 66*, *Twilight Zone*, and *The Outer Limits*. He has written a total of ten science fiction novels, among them *Costigan's Needle*, *The Altered Ego*, and *Night Slaves*, which became the second feature on *ABC Movie of The Week*.

Recently he turned to more serious fiction and has done three highly successful novels: *The Lemon Eaters*, *The Spun Sugar Hole*, and *The Resurrection of Frank Borchard*. He is also the author of a companion book to *Underhanded Bridge*—the recent humor hit, *Underhanded Chess*, also published by Hawthorn.

Mr. Sohl now lives in Thousand Oaks, California, with his wife (their children are grown) and a miniature Schnauzer named Buckminster who, Mr. Sohl insists, is smarter than he is.